It's *Show*time

Circus tricks: Learning
fun for horse and rider

It's *Show*time

Sylvia Czarnecki

Circus tricks: Learning
fun for horse and rider

The author and the publisher have collected the content of this book to their best knowledge and awareness. In case of any damage to humans or animals, occurring do to actions or decisions based on the information given by this book, no liability will be taken.

Imprint

Copyright © 2011 by Cadmos Verlag, Schwarzenbek
© This edition, 2015
Design: www.ravenstein2.de, Verden
Setting: Das Agenturhaus, Munich
Editor: Anneke Fröhlich

Cover Photograph: Karen Diehn
Photographs within the content without photo credit: Karen Diehn

Printing: Graspo CZ, a.s., Czech Republic, www.graspo.com

British Library Cataloguing in Publication Data.
A catalogue record of this book is available from the British Library.

Printed in Czech Republic

ISBN 978-0-85788-018-5

Contents

$\mathcal{C}$ontents

Circus tricks
Working systematically towards success

For quite some time now, the performance of circus tricks has not been limited to the circus big tops of the world. More and more people are discovering enjoyment in this unique and fascinating way of working with their horses. There is now barely a yard or equestrian centre in which at least one of its residents hasn't at the very least mastered the art of taking a bow.

Unfortunately, it is also obvious there is often a lack of structure or system when it comes to training these horses to perform circus tricks. Sometimes it is forgotten that we are dealing with a form of training that needs to be taken seriously. Just as in every other equestrian discipline, a solid and systematic approach is the key to you forging a harmonious relationship with your equine partner.

Working through circus-related lessons will bring enjoyment and variety into the daily routine. In addition to this, the classical circus lessons are particularly good as suppling exercises when correctly carried out. Bowing, kneeling, lying down,

Learning something new together, strengthening mutual bonds and having fun – working on circus tricks offers all these things.

sitting and the Spanish walk will all exercise the same multiple muscle groups that are used when horses are ridden or driven. Through the stretching and strengthening of tendons, ligaments and muscles, regular training will help to prevent injury and help avoid tension. The horse's balance is also trained, which means that circus trick training is also well suited to young or unbalanced horses.

The real benefit of circus work, however, is the way it helps both horse and handler to develop on a mental level. It stimulates communication, learning aptitude and trust, without the pressure or demand to perform. A horse that doesn't trust his trainer is unlikely to lie down in front of her. With time, the handler will find it easier to communicate with increasingly subtle signals and commands, and to work through new exercises.

By building up a correctlystructured training system, a horse can be encouraged to think with you, rather than just being a passive participant. Horses that master circus routines and tricks often have their own charisma and exude both confidence and vitality.

Required skills for horse and trainer

Being able to work horses in-hand with confidence is one of the prerequisites of successfully working through circus tricks. The basic skills of communication, understanding and respect should have been established already. The horse should alow himself to be touched everywhere, be happy to lift up his feet when asked, and accept being tied up. He must not be scared of the whip. The basics of being led in walk and trot on a straight line and on a circle, as well as halting, standing still, backing up and, ideally, lowering the head, should all pose no problems.

It is also advantageous if the horse is used to voice commands and understands being praised and reprimanded, so that you can give him the appropriate feedback and responses during work (such as 'that's right/wrong').

Having a trained eye with regard to the reactions and movement of your own horse is also important, so that you can act appropriately and make it as clear as possible to the horse what you would like from him. A slow, imprecise or uncoordinated response to a horse performing a desired movement, as well as the lack of praise, are all motivation-killers and will make the work unnecessarily difficult.

Of course, you can begin this work even if you can't fulfil all of these prerequisites. The training itself will quickly improve your skills in these areas too.

The horse's age

Providing a horse is used to people and has basic groundwork skills, circus training can be started with horses as early as two or three years of age. However, consideration should be given to a horse's individual

Before starting to work on circus routines, the horse should have been trained in basic groundwork.

stage of development. If a young horse absolutely refuses to carry out certain movements then – besides a lack of understanding – it could be due to a physical problem. Attention should also be paid to whether the horse is mentally mature enough to be able to concentrate and learn. This is rarely the case with a horse under two years of age. You run the risk of overfacing such a young horse by demanding too high a level of concentration from him.

This will not create a good basis for later training and can quickly lead to problems.

Horses find it easiest to learn when they are between two and six years of age, since the ability to learn and the instinct for play is especially pronounced at this stage. Additionally, a horse's natural curiosity at this age also makes work easier.

There is also nothing to be said against training horses to perform circus tricks when they are older or if they can't be ridden. Aslong as they are not physically constrained in their natural behaviours (rolling, lying down and so on) you need have no worries about demanding too much of them from a physical perspective. You should weigh up each case carefully, possibly also checking with your vet, in order to determine whether the work might be to the detriment of a horse's health. Whatever you do, in these circumstances, always proceed slowly. Older horses sometimes find it harder to learn new things or to do old things in a new way. Once you have got their interest in this new type of activity, they are usually enthusiastic participants!

The horse's breeding

Circus tricks are suitable for all breeds of horses. Some horses, however, will be particularly well or less well suited to certain tricks because of certain characteristics that

may be typical for their breed. Thorough-breds, for example, tend to be more highly-strung and will find exercises involving rearing or Spanish walk much easier than, for example, my own heavy horse Tarek, who by his very nature has a calmer temperament.

It is also possible to see how breeding affects a horse's learning behaviour. Horses who have draught breeding will learn in a markedly different way from Thoroughbreds. They often learn more

slowly and need longer to grasp what is wanted of them. If you put them under too much pressure, you can easily restrict their ability to think. Once they have learnt something however, they are very reliable and are attentive to and enjoy their work.

Warmbloods, on the other hand, will often learn faster but may tend to be over-motivated, which can make calm and con-centrated work more difficult. Since their flight instinct is more highly developed, they often need longer to learn exercises such as lying down or kneeling. This is outweighed, however, by the advantage gained on a mental level, which is all the greater.

Of course you cannot pigeonhole every horse like this. Just like people, horses are individuals and like to be treated as such.

Equipment and the training environment

Training equipment

It is important to wear sturdy footwear – this doesn't include wellingtons or trainers and certainly not sandals. It is always a possibility that your foot can accidently be trodden on. Gloves are also advisable in case your horse tries to pull the rope out of your hand or is startled by something. Avoid flapping or loose clothing, which might make it more difficult for your horse to read your body language correctly.

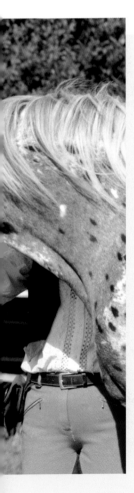

A varied education is not dependent on breeding.

Whip

The whip is an important communication tool and an essential part of your equipment. It serves as an extension of your arm. Used to supporti your signals, it will instinctively be understood by even young and inexperienced horses. It encourages, animates, confines, reminds, points the way and, in rare cases, it can also be used to reprimand. Depending on a horse's size, the whip should be between 80 and 120 cm long and not too flexible or 'whippy'. With a whip that is too springy or soft, it will be difficult to apply the precise and economical aids that are necessary.

White whips are clearly visible and have proven to be particularly effective. Whether you prefer a whip with a thong (the attachment at the end of the whip) or without is a matter of preference. I prefer the former, as my experience has shown that this type can be used with more precision. You should detach any hand straps or loops, as these can restrict your freedom of movement when using.

Head collar, rope and reins

A well-fitted head collar or rope halter is suitable for circus work, although a knotted rope halter can be slightly more severe in its effect. Avoid using a head collar with a stretch or elastic insert over the nose or poll as your horse may at the wrong moment be able to slip out of it surprisingly quickly and your aids will not be as controllable.

A correctly equipped horse and trainer pair

You should use a rope that has been specially designed for in-hand work. These are made from strong webbing or rope, and are woven around a core that gives the rope stability and the necessary weight.

The length should be between 3.5 and 3.8 metres and it should have a solid, compact clasp like a bull snap. Do not use one with a panic catch as these can be opened too quickly or accidentally, and usually at precisely the wrong moment. Lead ropes without a core or those made from cotton are as unsuitable as those made from polypropylene. They are too light, too thin and too loosely woven for you to be able to give your horse the subtle aids necessary for the training. A high quality rope has its price but this is the wrong place to try to save money.

If you need reins for an exercise, I would suggest you use rope reins becausethese will slide through your hands more easily than some leather reins will (especially those with some form of added grip). Alternatively you could use a long lead rope or normal reins that are attached to the head collar.

A bridle is only really an option when teaching the Spanish walk. In all other exercises and tricks, a head collar with reins or rope will be sufficient. You should really only turn to a bridle when you no longer require any form of rein aid to ask your horse to perform a specific trick.

The work space

Ensure you have a quiet and relaxing atmosphere and familiar surroundings in which to work. If you are not feeling right in yourself or if you are under stress, then it is best to postpone the training session to another day. Find a time when you will be able to work in peace and without interruption. You will move and act more confidently without spectators and in turn this will make communication between you and your horse significantly easier, esides which, both of you will be able to concentrate much better.

If possible, use an indoor school for the first few sessions – or at least a well-fenced arena or round pen in case your horse decides to try and make a premature exit.

The ground conditions also play an important role. The surface on which you are working should be as soft, as dry and as level as possible so that the horse is not put off and will be comfortable lying down.

The better the conditions are for training, the easier you will find it to work together. Try to make it as easy as possible for you and especially for your horse

!

A correctly-equipped horse and trainer combination.

A little bit of *L*earning theory

In recent times a lot has changed in the world of horse training. Previously, performance and success were the highest priority, but today the partnership and the enjoyment of the horse have moved to the fore. A partnership and the trust between horse and handler have to develop over time and cannotbe forced.

With the knowledge of a horse's natural behaviour and how it learns, it is possible to develop appropriate, stress-free and relaxed methods of training so that both horse and handler enjoy the work.

When working with living things three principles should always be considered. A creature can't'not learn', it can't 'not behave' and it can't 'not communicate'. Learning, behaving and communicating are conditions that are triggered as a result of reacting to stimuli and signals. Only those who are aware of this fact and keep it to the forefront of their thoughts can establish an appropriate training pro-

gramme and develop and ability to work effectively with their horses. On the following pages I will explain the process of how a horse learns and show you how we can influence this so that your training sessions work as well as possible and are enjoyable for both of you.

Survival depends on learning

Without the ability to learn, a horse would not be able to survive. For horses, learning is a lifelong process. A horse is continuously receiving a wide variety of stimuli through his sensory organs, which are then processed by the brain. It is there that the decision is made about the appropriate response.

Improving the equine condition

Horses do not learn in order to please someone else, but rather in order to make their own lives easier – that is what is meant by 'improving the equine condition'. It is therefore an incorrect assumption that a horse would do this or that in order to annoy you or anyone else. This is a purely human perception. This type of behaviour would make no sense at all for a horse as it would involve unnecessarily wasting vital energy.

If a horse does not do something when asked, or does it incorrectly, then there will always be a reason. Perhaps he hasn't understood what he is supposed to do or perhaps he is simply lacking in motivation. Your horse comes to a halt in the middle of the manège although you haven't finished the schooling session? He isn't doing this just to annoy you. Your horse probably associates the middle of the school with the ending of a training session and you, and only you, are responsible for this. By ending the lesson here the last three times of training your horse has learnt a new pattern of behaviour. He has associated the end of a training session with the middle of the manège. It is not for nothing that horses are described as creatures of habit.

Horses do not learn through understanding

Like most other creatures, horses learn by working through the required task and then consistently repeating what has been learnt. In contrast to us and a few other more highly developed species, the horse does not have the ability to truly 'understand'. His actions are primarily determined by instinct, previous experience or conditioned behaviour.

The process of 'learning through understanding' is shown by chimpanzees when, for example, sticks of bamboo are put in their cage for them to play with. If you were to put a banana down out of reach in front of their cage, then they are likely to use the stick sas an extension to their arms in order to fish for the banana and move it closer. A different experiment showed that apes stacked boxes on top of each other in their cage in order to reach a banana that had been hung out of reach above them. This research shows that primates are able to think logically.

Experiments into these so-called cognitive processes have been carried out with horses as well. Feed was placed on one side of a fence while a horse stood on the other side. If the horse were capable of cognitive reasoning, he would try to get through to the feed, instead of which he is likely to run up and down the fence line excitedly.

Despite this, we are often given the impression that in a human sense, a horse is

By using the approach and retreat method, a horse can learn to tolerate a plastic bag.

aware of his own actions. What is true, however, is that the reactions of a horse are not considered, conscious behaviour, but rather he has learnt through previous experience how to respond most appropriately to certain stimuli.

Learning theories

There is of course a variety of theories and methods by which a horse learns. Once we have understood them, and are able to implement them in training then we will be in a position to help our horses learn without stress.

Familiarisation

Familiarisation is one of the most frequently used and also one of the easiest theories of learning. A horse is faced repeatedly with the same stimulus. As a result, the horse's strength of reaction gradually reduces.

The method involving approach and retreat is linked with the principle of familiarisation, most easily explained using the example of a plastic bag. Most horses show fear or mistrust when faced with a plastic bag for the first time. If you want the horse to get used to it, then you bring the bag as close to the horse as possible without it causing him to run away. Whilst the bag may be at a sufficient distance for the moment, the horse is unlikely to tolerate it there for any length of time. For this reason, and to make it clear to the horse that the object isn't a permanent irritation, we need to use the method of approach and retreat. Move the plastic bag towards the horse and then take it away until the horse accepts it. The horse starts to get accustomed to the bag and the reaction shown by the horse will gradually lessen. You can then increase the difficulty by reducing the distance of the bag to the horse, touching the horse with the bag, or even waving it above the horse.

However, this process of familiarisation can also have a negative effect on a horse's training. If you flood the horse with too many stimuli without him really showing any reaction, or when the stimulus is too weak for it to cause a reaction, then famil-iarisation can have a blunting affect. This is often seen in riding school horses that hardly react or don't react at all to the rider's aids. This can be avoided by not continuously bombarding a horse with stimuli but rather using them only when you really expect or need a reaction. Any stimulus needs to be brief, concise and strong enough to provoke a response from the horse: as much as necessary but as little as possible.

In many forms of riding it is common practice for an aid to be given only when a new movement is required, and otherwise the rider remains passive. This assumes that the horse has learnt to remain engaged and active when the rider becomes passive. In point of fact, this is assumed to be the case in all of the most commonly found disciplines today. Sadly, and all too often, you see legs being used constantly to the extent that they soon have to squeeze every step out of the horse, leading to the horse becoming dead to the leg.

When familiarising a horse with anything, it is especially important to watch for the first signs of physical or mental tiredness. Any such signs will reduce the learning effect and can in certain circumstances have far-reaching mental consequences for the horse. If you put a saddle on a young horse for the first time and allow him to buck until he 'accepts' it then his acceptance is often more down to physical exhaustion than to the horse getting used to the feel of the saddle. You are more likely to develop mistrust on the side of the horse rather than any sign of familiarisation. The consequences of such a mis-

!

Familiarisation to a stimulus will lead to the horse's sensitivity threshold being lowered, leading to a gradual weakening of his reaction.

For an aid to be given correctly it needs to be applied precisely and with restraint. Constant nagging with the leg will deaden a horse to the aids.

judgement are likely to be felt throughout the training as the horse's ability to trust will have been damaged so that the horse is likely to approach any new exercises with suspicion.

Alongside a horse's own experience, the reaction of other horses also plays a significant role. If the majority of a herd set off and run away from a relatively harmless source of danger such as flapping tarpaulin, even the horse that is used to plastic tarpaulins is going to be pulled along with the rest of the herd. In this case, instincts and the link with the behaviour of the rest of the herd outweigh anything else.

On the other hand, the behaviour of other horses can be put to positive use. If a horse is scared of walking through water then it is often enough to have a more experienced horse go in front so that the horse overcomes his own mistrust, relies on the experience of the other horse and follows. The calming influence of other horses can also be a great help. A horse that gets anxious in atrailer can be put next to a good traveller to get used to travelling by this means.

One-off familiarisation of a horse to a new stimulus is not enough. This process is generally accepted to be reversible, meaning that the newly acquired knowledge needs to be regularly refreshed in order for the horse to maintain his state of familiarisation. This also means however that a single negative experience is sufficient for the horse's basic instinct to kick in and the learned behaviour to be wiped out.

Classical conditioning

Ivan Pavlov carried out probably the most significant experiments into classical conditioning with his research into conditioned reflexes. Unconditional responses are unbreakable circuits fixed deep in the brain, which you cannot immediately and deliberately influence. An example of this is that you will blink quickly and without thinking about it when something comes towards your eye. Conditioned responses, however, are learned. In the case of classical conditioning, the unconditional stimulus that sets off the trigger mechanism is replaced with a new, so-called 'conditioned' stimulus. A new signal is thus linked with an already familiar action or reaction, and after the conditioning, this signal by itself will cause the reaction.

In the stable yard, classical conditioning can be seen most commonly at daily feeding time. The sound of the feed bins becomes the signal thatfeeding is about to happen. After some time, the sound itself will be enough for the horse to start producing gastric juices. This is not just dependent on the signal but also on the situation and the surroundings. The gastric juices will start to be produced when all factors occur simultaneously, but not if the horse hears the sound of the bins when he is being schooled rather than standing in his box.

Operant conditioning

Also known as instrumental learning, operant conditioning is very similar to the classical form. The expression 'instrumental' refers to the fact the behaviour is the instrument or means thatcauses the corresponding action or consequence. A specific type of behaviour can be shaped by the consequence or consistent action that follows it. Depending on the type of reinforcement, the behaviour will be shown either more or less often – or can even be totally erased (no longer shown). This type of learning is also referred to as 'trial and error' or 'learning by success'. A distinction is made between four different types of reaction, introduced below.

Positive reinforcement

Everything associated with an action that contributes to it being repeated is characteristic of positive reinforcement. A specific behaviour is followed immediately by a positive, pleasant consequence for the horse, such as being given food. If you regularly reinforce the action of a horse lowering his head with food then he will drop his head in order to receive the reward. The greater the incentive and the intensity of the praise, the greater the motivation will be. This will result in the behaviour being

In the theory of positive reinforcement, a horse volunteers an action – here, lowering his head on command from a movement of the handler's hand. By showing the correct behaviour he is rewarded – preferably with food.

repeated by the horse more reliably and more frequently. In this the horse is no different from us humans.

This form of reinforcement is a very powerful one, since the learning process is not influenced by unpleasant stimuli (stress, aggression or force) and the horse exhibits the behaviour of his own free will. Unlike classical conditioning, the horse performs the action himself and can therefore influence the consequences of his own actions. This active participation in the course of events has in itself a similarly powerful effect and acts extremely positively on the horse's mind.

Negative reinforcement

In the case of negative reinforcement, a negative stimulus stops as soon as the behaviour is changed in a positive or desirable way. Following the principle of positive reinforcement, I can teach a horse to lower his head by waiting until he lowers his head of his own volition and then reinforcing this action. Alternatively, I can use a negative reinforcement method by exerting pressure on the horse's poll until he gives way to the pressure and drops his

In the case of negative reinforcement, the horse is rewarded by the removal of an unpleasant stimulus as soon as he changes his behaviour in the desired way. If the horse drops his head then the pressure on his poll is released.

head to escape the pressure. As soon as he drops his head, the stimulus (the pressure on the poll) disappears, which reinforces the horse's action. He learns that it is better to lower his head in order to avoid the pressure.

A horse will learn just as quickly and reliably to change his behaviour through the use of negative reinforcement. However, for the horse the real motivation to want to change behaviour and the incentive of knowing it is worth doing something is greater in the case of positive reinforcement.

There is nothing to be said against praising the horse when he shows the correct reaction, and thus giving him additional motivation. From a scientific perspective, however, this does not turn negative reinforcement into a positive one.

Positive punishment

When we speak about punishment then positive punishment is usually referred to because it involves the application of a negative, unpleasant stimulus. It is, unfortu- nately, the most commonly used method of stopping an unwanted form of behaviour, or rather reducing the incidence of it occurring, even though in most cases it is relatively ineffectual.

It is said that for a punishment (just as with praise) to be effective, so that a horse understands its purpose, it must happen within at least three seconds of the undesirable behaviour or action happening. Any later and it is ineffective, because the horse no longer makes the connection between the two.

Often a behaviour is only weakened or suppressed through punishment. It is not uncommon, however, for a horse to simply learn to be shrewder. If your horse goes to nip you and is told off for it, then next time it is likely that he will just be more careful either not to be caught or to dodge the reprimand. As a result, he will wait until you have turned your back (thus putting him out of reach of punishment) and then nip you. If you then punish him, it will probably be too late. If you get to the horse in time with your reprimand, then next time he will be likely to nip someone else when you aren't there. That person will probably be toosurprised will beto be able to tell the horse off within the necessary time frame, but the horse is still given attention (social contact). Social contact is a primary (in-born and not acquired through learning) reinforcement and thus the horse is in effect being rewarded for his bad behaviour. As a result, he will continue to nip. Punishment is therefore only effective at any and every sign of the unwanted behaviour – and who can be with their horse twenty-four hours a day? Consequentially, when being punished, a horse is only receiving a part of the information, namely that this behaviour is wrong, and not how he can change or what the correct behaviour would be. It is therefore only logical that when the horse shows the right behaviour he should be positively reinforced, rather than us waiting to punish the wrong behaviour.

By persistently punishing a horse for an action without showing him the correct alternative, he will quickly become confused or worried. This applies just as much to aggression directed towards horses (punishment is a form of aggression) that they don't understand, as is the case when they are punished for doing something for which they are usually praised. Equally, punishment for a behaviour that a horse couldn't understand as being wrong, such as bucking or rearing as a result of pain, can lead to increased confusion. The stress reaction that causes these actions also inhibits the learning process in the brain. For this reason, stress should be avoided at all costs. A further problem with punishment, which should not be underestimated, is the so-called 'learned helplessness'. A horse that is exclusively trained using punishment will at some stage no longer be able to learn anything new. He will have lost all of his motivation and curiosity for trying out anything new, so that – to be on the safe side – he will only exhibit behaviour that he is certain will not result in punishment.

Negative punishment or eradication

Negative punishment means that something the horse enjoys or finds pleasant is taken away or doesn't occur. Neither positive nor negative reinforcement is given to an action, but rather it is simply ignored. This method can also be used to undo an already learned behaviour. If the positive stimulus isn't given and there is therefore no motivation for the horse to perform an action, then, the action may still be repeated but gradually the desire to do it will reduce and the behaviour will not happen at all – it is erased.

Ignoring a horse can in certain circumstances have the effect of a punishment. This equates to attention and social contact being withheld from the horse. (Photo: Gabi Appelt)

Certain behaviour can be self-reinforcing. Many horses love standing on a pedestal so much that ignoring them as a form of negative punishment has no effect as long as there remains any opportunity for the horse to climb up onto the pedestal.

When a behaviour is erased, this doesn't mean that it will never happen again. Ignoring – which is the classical form of negative punishment – will only work in the case of unconscious (un-learned) behaviour when it is consistently applied. If the behaviour is exhibited again and is then unconsciously reinforced through attention given to the horse, it will happen again.

Some forms of behaviour cannot be removed using this method, since it is self-reinforcing. A horse that constantly neighs or calls because he lacks company won't stop if he is ignored, since this behaviour is self-reinforcing. This means that the horse is rewarding himself with his be-

haviour. This is just as much the case when a horse likes the 'view' he gets when mounting a platform – he won't stop doing it just because he isn't given praise.

A good example of how negative punishment works is the case of a small child and his or her parents. Usually, small children will start to whine when they want to be given a particular toy. Whining is a learned behaviour since most parents resist for a certain amount of time but then eventually give in and buy the child the toy. This behaviour has therefore been reinforced and the child has learned something: 'I only have to whine for long enough to get what I want'. In theory, it is simple to reverse this behaviour just by ignoring it. But I am sure that you know yourself how difficult this is in reality. Your own action in giving way to the child has been reinforced because his or her whining has stopped. The child was given negative reinforcement and whined until he got his own way. Ignoring it is an effective way of stopping the whining, so be strong!

Imitation

Imitation is also known as 'learning by watching', which is rather a good way of describing this type of learning. A living being learns to copy visually observed or aurally-absorbed patterns of behaviour. A foal learns to drink water and eat grass by copying his mother and the other horses in the herd, these abilities only being instinctive to a limited extent. Imitation can also be used in training, especially to master situations unknown to a horse. If you let an experienced horse go first, then a younger animal often only needs to be asked and he will cross the 'danger zone'.

For foals, imprinting starts immediately after birth.

Imprinting

Imprinting is viewed as a special form of learning. It always takes place in a set timescale specific to the species: in the case of a newborn foal, this timeframe is between half an hour and a maximum of two days. As a rule, imprinting tends to lead to an irreversible change in behaviour.

One important form of imprinting in newborn foals is object imprinting. Here a foal learns to recognise his mother and, thus, his own species through external influences. Since a foal doesn't know what it is at birth. there can be fatal consequences if contact between him and his mother is interfered with. A foal that does

27

The key to mutual success lies in your horse's motivation.

not have social contact with other horses immediately after birth, and in his first stages of life, will often have lifelong problems in recognising others of his own species.

Principle: motivation through reward

We now know how learning and teaching works in theory. In practice, however, the individual types of learning are not always so clearly separable and will often flow seamlessly from one into the other. A horse will do something for two reasons: because he expects something positive, or wants to avoid something negative. This principle is known as motivation through reward.

Which type of reinforcement is the 'better' one, the negative or the positive, is not always so easy to identify. You should always only use as much pressure as necessary to achieve a result. When you see any opportunity to use no pressure at all and your horse is able to find his own way of achieving what you want, take full advantage of this. However, positive reinforcement is not always the most effective means. Numerous attempts to guess what the point of the exercise is, without your horse receiving any positive response from you, can lead to unnecessary frustration andhe will eventually justgive up. Sometimes it makes more sense to make it clear to your horse what it is that you want. Listen to your horse and to your own intuition when pressure becomes force. It is important that you reward even the smallest of steps.

Using feed as a reward

Basically, you can use anything that your horse is prepared to work for as a reward. It may not necessarily be something that you would think of as a reward. A distinction can be made between two types of praise: primary and secondary reinforcement.

A so-called positive (primary) reinforcement is anything a horse really likes and for which he is prepared to do something to earn. In other words, the prospect of receiving this positive reinforcement will act as a motivating factor forthe horse. Primary means the horse doesn't first need to learn that the reinforcement is positive. Included in this category are feed, sexual drive, rolling, contact withhis companions in the field, playing and movement. Since we can't let our horse go out and play with his paddock mates every time he does something well, feed is ideally suited as primary reinforcement. The need to ingest feed is a basic necessity for horses, which is why feed is of such importance.

Ensure you always have treats within easy reach. A belt bag or a jacket with big pockets are both well suited to the task.

The so-called secondary reinforcements are, for example, praise with touch or voice. They tend not to have such as strong an effect as primary reinforcement, since a horse has to learn their meaning through conditioning.

In my daily work, using feed as a reward is a matter of course. Why shouldn't I use the strongest motivator available to me? Training with treats is often criticised, since it has the reputation of training a horse to beg. This isn't down to the fact that titbits are given as reward, but rather is due to

Feeding politely

Horses familiar with the system of reward as described can be given a small treat in between times. If they are not so well trained, giving a treat without reason can mean you have to go back to the start. Those who give horses treats just for the sake of it shouldn't be surprised if their horses then beg for them.

To train politeness when receiving treats, you can teach your horse to 'look away'. If your horse is very pushy, position him behind a fence or stable door to maintain your own personal space. Hold the treat in your hand so that your horse registers it but can't reach it. Now wait. As soon as your horse turns his head away, reinforce this by saying your praise word and give him the treat. If there are no problems in doing this behind the barrier, then practice it without a barrier. Position yourself in front of your horse and hold out the treat just as before in one hand, with the end of the lead rope in the other. If your horse gets pushy and tries to invade your space or tries to grab the treat, wiggle the rope to make it clear he has to stop. Don't react prematurely if you think

Take particular care from the start that your horse remains polite when being fed his treat. To help with this, you can teach your horse to turn his head away from the treat before he gets it.

your horse is going to get pushy, but rather allow him to make the mistake. The horse has to know what is going to happen before it happens. Only then can your reaction be recognised by the horse as a consequence of his action. If he remains pushy, go back behind a fence until your horse has understood that he will only get his treat when he looks away.

If you like, you can also give link the action with a command (eg 'look away') so that you can ask for it on command and differentiate it from other exercises.

the way the trainer uses and gives the feed to the horse. To avoid your horse starting to beg for treats, it is necessary to incorporate rewarding with feed into a clearly understandable system for the horse. He has to learn that only correct behaviour will result in a reward.

It is sensible to extend this chain with another link. Think up a word of praise that will make it clear to your horse that the behaviour or action shown was desirable and correct. Always ensure you use the same word, so that your horse becomes conditioned to it and learns its meaning and association. This is similar to clicker training, in which the sound of the clicker is a sign to the horse that his reaction was correct, so the horse connects the 'click of praise' with the reward. This makes it easier to reinforce your horse's action at exactly the right time and to gain a bit of time until giving the actual treat. It would be wrong to omit giving a treat when your horse has done what you have asked of him. The use of your word of praise or the clicker is a promise to the horse. 'What you have done was correct and so you will now get your treat'. This ensures your horse stays permanently motivated and trusts your praise.

If you keep consistently to these rules you should be able to prevent any form of begging. Of course, the horse does need to learn how the system works. In certain circumstances it might take a while until your horse really takes you seriously and understands that you won't give in and give him a treat before he has completed his task (think about the example of the whining child).

Make it as easy for your horse as possible by putting him in the best start position for each exercise.

Preparing for and working through a training session

A successful training session is dependent on having a plan in mind. How do I start an exercise? How do I work through it? How should it run? Before beginning, you should be aware of a few basic things:

- Always put your horse in a good starting position, from which he will be able to easily carry out your instructions. In the case of the bow, for example, ensure the horse is standing with the forelegs as far forward and as wide apart as possible.

From this position he will be able to carry out your instructions (putting his head down between his legs) easily and won't get frustrated during his first attempts because he doesn't understand and can't do what you are asking of him.

- Break each exercise down into as many small steps as possible. In your mind sketch out the individual learning steps so you have a clear picture of what you are trying to get across to your horse. Set the bar low enough that your horse can carry out your instructions easily, and then increase the difficulty only when you are sure he has understood the previous steps. By doing this, you will have lots of 'mini' successes on the way to the completed exercise with sufficient opportunities to praise your

It is important to have a clear picture of the exercise in your head so you can give the precise aids needed. This becomes more important as your horse learns more commands.

horse. Don't be afraid of going back a few steps if you encounter difficulties. It is all too easy for step two to happen accidentally before step one, without the horse really understanding how he got there or what he was actually supposed to do.

• Think of a clear, unmistakable voice command. Avoid it being too similar to voice commands that you already use. The command 'back' may sound similar to your horse to 'walk'. He may in time learn to recognise the fine difference – but why should we make it even harder than it might already be? As soon as your horse understands the exercise, repeat the command frequently before and whilst practicing. This is how your horse learns to connect the exercise with the command. Later, you

should only give the command at the start of the exercise and only repeat it if necessary. The goal is for the horse to carry out the exercise or trick on one command.

When you begin, the signal you give is more important than the voice command. It is the signal that is really the aid. A horse isusually quick to connect a visual or physical cue with an exercise. This cue is normally given with a whip. Since the horse's legs are often inundated with touching aids, you need to be particularly precise in order to prevent confusion. Again, once learnt, the horse should only need to be asked once for him to carry out the exercise. In both cases these are called 'control cues'.

Every exercise needs to have a clear end. The word 'up' is particularly well suited for all those exercises in which the horse stands in an unusual position, such as with the bow, so long as you aren't already using it for another exercise (eg, 'Get up').

After performing each exercise correctly – for the level of training – the horse should be praised or given a treat. If the horse carries out the exercise worse than usual then there should be no reward and the exercise should be repeated. This stimulates the horse's 'ambition' and gives him the incentive to try harder next time. If he goes on to perform the exercise satisfactorily the next time then he should be even better rewarded.

Always take a break from, or end the training when the horse has been particularly good and you aren't expecting any further improvement to be made. If, after several tries, the horse steadily gets worse rather than better, try going back to something easier or something the horse particularly enjoys doing, and return to the more difficult task at a later point. Even if there is little or no improvement on the last attempt at the exercise, for the sake of your horse, end it there and look forward to a better session next time.

Clicker training

One way of learning that is particularly well suited to the training covered in this book is clicker training. You can, of course, successfully work without a clicker, but it is helpful when it comes to the training of tricks and there is a multitude of ways in which it can be used. If you are interested, there are many good books and courses that can help you learn how to work with the clicker.

I have already outlined how horses learn and how to praise them correctly: only correct behaviour results in verbal praise and then a feed reward. If you keep using this sequence, you aren't very far from working in the same way clicker training does – you would simply replace the noise of the clicker with your voice as the marker of correct behaviour. In other words, correct behaviour results in a click and then a treat. Additionally, every exercise also has a clear end.

The little box's advantage over your voice is its unmistakable sound. It is clearly different from any other of the background noises around you and is clearly recognisable in every situation. For your pupil, the clicker

Clickers are practical to use and can be found in pet stores next to the dog training accessories.

For tricks such as 'snatching the cap from the head', the clicker is ideal as an aid.
(Photo: Gabi Appelt)

itself means: 'What you have just done at the precise moment I clicked was right and you will be rewarded.' It can be used much more quickly than your voice, allowing you to give reinforcement to the exact second for an action or reaction.

After appropriate conditioning, the click triggers expectation in your horse, so that you have a few more seconds of time to give him a treat. The click is a promise to your horse that a feed reward follows as a result of him reacting in the correct way. You should maintain this approach in the case of more advanced work, as the clicker serves not as a replacement for praise but rather simply as notification that it will follow.

Exact timing with the clicker leads to a horse very quickly grasping what we want from him. As a result of successfully learning new things, the horse's motivation will increase, which in turn leads to faster learning. By using the clicker a particular response can be established within a few hours or often even minutes, which would take possibly weeks or months to achieve using more traditional methods.

In order to work using a clicker you need to go through a conditioning process with your horse. It is easiest to do this by training something simple and reinforcing every correct reaction with a click, immediately followed by a treat. A lesson such as 'pick up' (see page 125) is well suited for this purpose. Once the clicker has been established in the training process, it is an outstanding tool for training tricks.

*E*ntering
the world of the circus

To get you and your horse ready for training and to prepare your horse's muscles for the tasks ahead, you should always conscientiously go through a warm-up. In addition to learning a variety of stretching and loosening exercises, the mountain goat exercise and bowing are, besides their suppling properties on account of their level of difficulty, ideal ways of entering the world of the circus.

Warming up, stretching and feeding techniques

The horse's musculoskeletal system is extremely sensitive. The muscles and ligaments in the neck and back are particularly susceptible to injury. For this reason you should start the actual work only when your horse has been able to stretch and has been warmed up properly.

Begin by leading your horse round in walk a few times and then in trot. Be creative and don't just stay on the outside track. Try circles and serpentines, and don't forget to change the rein. Changes within the pace and backing up correctly help strengthen the communication between you and your horse and also support muscle development.

Utilise the warm-up effectively and use it to train some of the basic lessons, such as halting, standing still, stepping back and following. Once the muscles are loosely warmed up you can begin with some of the stretching exercises.

As well as serving to prevent injury, the preliminary stretching exercises will also extend your horse's range of movement and teach co-ordination and a greater awareness of the body for both horse and handler. It is not just the horse that should learn how to move correctly in this preparatory phase – you also need to learn the correct movement patterns so that they have become routine by the time you get to the more advanced work.

Another very important aspect of the stretching exercises is how you position the treats in your hand so that your horse is encouraged into a particular outline. In most cases you would be advised to offer a long carrot in such a way that your fingers stay safe, just as I have written in the past. Between initially writing this book and this revised edition, I have worked with a lot of horses and have seen repeatedly that – although my fingers stay safe – the horse develops bad habits or simply goes after the feed but doesn't really concentrate on

what he does to get it. Since a horse expects the carrot but can't see it, after several repetitions the horse often starts to get increasingly frenetic or rushed so that he no longer has any control over the sequence of movement. Besides, this type of behaviour works contrary to learning to accept feed politely. Instead of relying on a carrot that your horse finds his own way to, start to teach your horse to lock on to your hand as the source of the treat. With this I mean the horse maintains contact with your hand and follows its movement. You should always have the feeling that your horse is pushing your hand into the desired position. Admittedly, this technique requires a certain amount of practice until is perfected, but it brings many benefits.

Locking on to the hand that feeds

Place the treat into the palm of your hand and cup your hand around it to hold it in place without putting your fingers at risk. Work out the right size of treat for this and practice holding it before working with your horse!

Stretching the top line, for a strain in the neck. (Photos: Berit Seiboth)

Freeing up the poll and stretching the top line

First of all, stand on your horse's left side and put a treat (as just described) in the right hand. Stand at your horse's shoulder, looking straight ahead so you can place your hand lengthwise under the horse's mouth. Begin by standing far enough forward so your horse has to stretch slightly. Put your hand under his mouth and wait until your horse tries to take the treat out of your hand. If your horse is rude or tries to snatch, hold his head over your feed hand by placing your left hand on his halter. When the horse's mouth makes contact with your hand, move your hand slightly back so the horse lifts his poll. This will happen if you keep your hand at the same level as you draw it back, even if the horse tries to push it down. Only when the horse is in the position you want should you use your marker

39

3

The horse needs to learn to take up a polite contact with the palm of your hand. He can move his lips but should not bite. (Photo: Berit Seiboth)

signal and give him the treat by opening your hand. This exercise is fairly demanding, but it is important if you want to progress further. If you move your hand back too early and in effect 'run away' from your horse's mouth, your horse will try to be quicker than you to get his treat. You really need to practice this exercise thoroughly. The horse needs to learn to take up and maintain a definite but polite contact with your hand. Once you have stretched the muscles through the neck and poll, you then need to bring the horse's mouth more in the direction of his chest, so that the

To stretch the top line, tempt your horse to drop his head towards his chest.

horse's top-line is also stretched. Ensure the exercise is carried out in as slowly and controlled a way as possible, and with the starting point far enough in front of the horse. Put your hand containing the treat to the horse's mouth only if the horse remains polite and he doesn't beg or snatch, otherwise you will just reinforce this behaviour. Wait until he holds his head still and is standing quietly, even if this takes some time.

You should do this exercise from both sides since both types of bowing, the one- and two-legged variants, will be trained from both sides as well.

Lateral Mobility

To work on the lateral mobility of the poll stand next to your horse and put one hand on the bridge of the horse's nose positioned slightly on the offside on top of the head-collar. Put the other hand on the horse's lower jaw. Create flexion through the poll by supporting the lower jaw with one hand and bring the horse's nose around towards you with the other. You don't need a lot of flexion, rather you should aim for a loosening and 'giving' through the poll. Don't use too much pressure but instead wait until the horse relaxes and then, if necessary, ask for a bit more flexion. Next you should stretch the neck muscles along the neck. This time, stand in front of the horse and

Lateral mobility through the poll: the horse's neck remains straight. (Photos: Berit Seiboth)

hold on to the head collar on each side of the head. Move around until you are on a level with the horse's shoulder, ensuring you keep sufficient distance and achieve an angle of 90 degrees. If you went further and asked for more bend, the poll would rotate and this would put unnecessary strain on other muscles. If your horse doesn't want to stand still when you are doing this, try standing further away from his shoulder so that you give him enough room to stretch out his neck, and try doing the exercise more slowly. It is better to praise earlier for achieving less bend than waiting until the horse makes a mistake. Remember, you may need to practice this before your horse can stretch as far round as 90 degrees.

Lateral mobility of the neck: the horse bends his neck through an angle of up to 90 degrees. (Photos: Berit Seiboth)

When stretching the front legs, it is advantageous if the horse supports himself on your hand, to enable him to achieve an extension through the leg and shoulder. (Photo: Berit Seiboth)

Stretching the fore and hind limbs

The next exercise serves to stretch both the forelegs and the shoulder as well as the anterior muscles of the back.

Stand at an angle in front of your horse, in case your horse moves his front leg a little bit too vigorously. Stroke your right hand down the back of the horse's leg and hold the back of the horse's hoof below the pastern to enable you to stretch it gently towards you. Wait until the horse stretches the leg forwards of his own accord. Maintain it briefly and then put the leg down. If your horse doesn't co-operate,use your left hand to tug the head collar slightly forwards to encourage him to stretch. Thisactive stretching is especially effective and, in terms of the length of the stretch, is very close to the movement desired in the one- and two-legged bow. Under no circum-stances should you lift the leg up to the horizontal or pull it – you are trying to stretch the shoulder and this would only be made more difficult if there was any rotation of the shoulder blade, which would also result in the back dropping.

Next, move to the horse's hindleg, holding it in the same place behind the foot and pull it carefully forwards under his body, towards the front foot. Avoid any sideward movement to the outside, since this will result in an unwanted rotation through the hip joint. This stretching movement is, unlike the stretch through the shoulder, more passive in nature – meaning that it relies on you to create the stretch.

Now stand beside your horse's hindquarters, as if you were going to pick out his hind foot. Hold onto the hoof with your right hand and put the other hand onto the hock. Pick up the hoof and pull it back

Stretching the muscles in the hindquarters forwards and backwards. (Photos: Berit Seiboth)

slightly until you are stretching it gently. Be aware of your own safety and don't put yourself into the danger zone immediately behind your horse.

Stretching the muscles down the horse's side and through the shoulder

The last exercise before we turn to the 'real' circus tricks involves stretching the muscles down the horse's side and torso, bringing the shoulder into this again. Here too you use treats in your hand to encourage the horse to move his head around towards his knee.

Position yourself next to your horse and bring the horse's head around in a curve at a height level with his point of shoulder until his mouth is as close to his knee joint as possible. The inside foreleg should move slightly back to ensure that the horse can stretch fully down his side.

To stretch the lateral hind muscles and the shoulder bring your horse's head round towards his hock.

If the horse tries to move his quarters around at the first attempt, check your position. If necessary, you could position your horse next to a fence or the side of the school to stop this happening.

The mountain goat exercise

For the mountain goat exercise, the horse needs to move his hindlegs closer forwards to the fore legs, putting them under his centre of gravity. At the same time he will need to drop his head and neck. This exercise was developed in the nineteenth century and was considered to stretch the entire top line and hindquarters, and is beneficial for the training of every horse. It is a useful tool for learning other tricks throughout your horse's circus training career.

*C*hecklist

Required skills for the mountain goat exercise

- Standing still
- Respect for, but no fear of, the whip
- If possible, the horse should have the ability to drop his head

For this exercise I would recommend you plait your horse's tail and possibly also turn it up and bandage it. This will help you to avoid catching his tail with your whip when touching the hindlegs, and it will also allow your horse to pick up your signals more easily.

It is essential the horse is used to the whip and neither ignores it nor is scared of it. In addition, he should have learned to stand still. You could have a second person to hold the horse but personally I don't think this should be necessary since the horse should concentrate solely on you and the signals you are giving him during the exercise.

To start, position your horse so that he is standing with the forelegs parallel to each other. Since you want to move the hindlegs more underneath the horse, towards his centre of gravity, it is advantageous if the hindlegs are not square when learning this trick. You should stand facing the horse on the side that has his hindleg positioned further back, and hold the whip so it is pointing back towards the hindleg.

Now stroke the horse's croup from top to bottom with the whip and down the hindlegs, until you get to the back of the cannon bone. Tap it here gently and give the appropriate voice command. I use the word 'forwards' because I think it makes sense that the horse learns the difference between moving his legs forwards and backwards. If he reacts by lifting his leg, praise him generously – he has just learned the first step. If your horse doesn't react, vary your touching aid in either strength or rhythm, or use feed to get him to drop his head a bit. This causes a degree of tension over his top line and encourages the horse to step forwards. At some stage, your horse will react in some way – even if just with a twitch of a muscle which is precisely the moment to praise him. You will see that with praise and the right timing, what starts as a twitch of muscle will soon become the lifting of a leg. Once your

As a first step, the horse learns to lift his leg at the touch of the whip.

As the exercise develops, the horse is praised for moving his hindlegs forwards.

horse confidently reacts with a lifting of his leg to your touch of the whip – and it might not happen on the same day but is more likely after several training sessions – change the way you give him praise. You should start to praise him only when he actually moves his leg forwards, regardless of how many centimetres of movement in that direction. If he lifts his leg but puts it down further back, he should not be praised.

As a rule, the horse always leaves the leg that he has placed forwards in place – so this is your next job. The simplest way to do this is by getting him to move his weight onto the leg he has moved underneath it. Put your hand on your horse's quarters, move around the horse and rock it gently to the side on which he has moved the hind-leg forwards. If the horse is still happily standing quietly, touch the other leg (on the side you are now standing) in the same way and ask this one to be moved forward. Follow the same process as you did with the other leg, teaching him to move forward and then take up the weight.

If you horse moves his leg back before you have a chance to change sides and get

him to shift his weight over, simply carry out the same step again but reach over his quarters and pull gently towards you to get him to shift his weight.

Once your horse has moved both legs forwards, end the lesson by asking your horse to take a clear step forward and then start again once he has taken a few strides.

If, after a few training sessions, your horse is happy to move his legs forwards in response to your touch, next ask him to lower his head by offering him feed low down in front of his forelegs. If your horse has already been taught to lower his head you may only need to give the appropriate command. Most horses will usually drop their heads when doing the mountain goat exercise, since they find it more comfortable to do this when stretching the top line. If the head is held higher, then this can cause the back to hollow and put more strain on the shoulders.

There are both anatomical and theoretical learning reasons why a horse should be taught to move his legs underneath his centre of gravity by himself and not rely on a signal from your hand or a leg rope to do this. The horse has to be aware of the sequence of movements in order to be able to carry this out well. From this stage on, it is a matter of practicing until you see clear signs of progress. Depending on how well you are able to motivate and encourage the horse, enabling him to be able to follow your

It could take many months for your horse to be able to perform the mountain goat exercise to the level of perfection shown here by Santano with Sarah.

Little helpers

An optical barrier can help some horses to understand and learn how to perform the mountain goat exercise. Put two poles on the ground, parallel to each other, and place the horse so that in the starting position his forelegs are behind the front pole and his hindlegs are behind the second pole. Touch the hindlegs and ask the horse to lift and place them down in front of the back pole. For horses that are familiar with walking over tyres and are used to placing their feet inside them, these too can be used to help learning. A horse might find the required amount of stretching strenuous in this position so don't ask him to maintain the position for too long. If your horse is happy and confident in standing on a platform, you can also use this to work on this exercise – provided the platform is big enough and not too high. You would not want your horse to hurt himself in the early stages when he is still learning.

!

instructions, you should quickly become successful. For the final few centimetres when the fore and hindlegs get closer together or even almost touch, you will need some time. This requires a high degree of stretching, which a horse needs time to develop.

The two-legged bow / Pliè

In the two-legged bow (also called plié) the horse lowers himself back and down over his outstretched forelegs. You often see a similar movement when a horse is stretching. You see similar behaviour in foals when they are stretching down to eat grass, as their forelegs are relatively long in relation to the length of their necks.

The bow exercises a variety of muscles. It places particular demands on the horse's top line. The nuchal ligament, which in riding plays a significant role, is tensed and the spine is stretched in such a way that the space between each vertebra is opened up. Depending on how far and for how long the horse stretches back and down, which also makes him push back through his quarters, the muscle in the croup and quarters will also be given a work out.

Since the bow is relatively easy to train and is also one of the prerequisites for the one legged bow, it is well suited as an introduction to circus work. Once the horse has got the hang of the two-legged bow it won't take long to learn how to do a good-looking one-legged bow, since the sequence of movements is very similar.

Preparation – putting in 'park'

Whatever you try to teach your horse, always aim to make it as simple as possible. By doing this you will avoid any frustration and succeed not just more rapidly but also with a much happier and better motivated horse.

In the case of the bow, this principle means that you should begin with the horse in what we call the 'park' position. The forelegs should be positioned as far in front of the hindlegs as possible, and wide enough for it to be easy for the horse to put his head down between them. If you don't start from this position, your horse is likely to shift his weight onto his toes and bend the forelegs, which is to be avoided at all costs. Bending the forelegs shifts the weight in the wrong direction and leads to the horse working downwards instead of backwards. It can also cause him to lose his balance or even fall over. Also remember that the bow isn't a downwards movement but rather a backwards one.

To practice moving into the bowing position, you need to teach the horse to move the forelegs bit by bit forwards in turn. He will need to move each leg forward, one and then the other, in very small steps. The smaller the steps, the less you have to use your hands to position the legs and the more independently your horse can work, then the sooner the horse will learn to stand correctly and carry out the exercise without any problems. I always use feed to encourage the horse to move his forelegs into position, since I find this the quickest way of training a horse to perform the required movement.

Take tiny steps and generously reward. Once the horse knows what the signal is that tells him to move his feet forwards, reduce the treats and give them once the horse is in position with his feet extended out.

If the bow is well prepared, the horse should lower himself down and back through his outstretched front legs. (Photos: Berit Seiboth)

Position yourself in front of your horse, hold onto his halter with the hand closest to his head, and move his head slightly away from you – just far enough to make it easier for him to shift his weight. With your other hand, run it down the back of the leg that is now not bearing as much weight as before. Start at the top, directly underneath the elbow, and run your hand down to the bottom with a bit of pressure and vigour – not slowly or cautiously. Most horses will respond by automatically lifting or moving the leg forwards. As the horse goes to put the foot down use the halter to move the horse towards you so that he puts his weight onto that leg. If this doesn't happen, lift and move the leg forward by hand.

The moment he puts his weight on to the leg he has just moved, generously praise your horse, regardless of how small that step was. Pay attention to your timing and only offer praise when the horse puts weight down on to that foot. If your horse moves the leg back again when you change sides, try to keep his head in position using the halter. If the horse drops his head or bends it round too much this can encourage him to move his hindlegs forwards in error.

Over time and with confidence you will be able to replace the use of your hand with the whip and use this to stroke down the back of the forelegs. It is important, however, to differentiate how and where you use it in this exercise in comparison with other similar commands you might use.

If the horse is correctly in position, allow your horse to 'lock on' to your hand and tempt his mouth down towards his chest. Hold the treat in front of his chest until he has shifted his weight back, and reward this several times.

The bow takes shape

The next step is to put your hand on the horse's chest from behind through his

At the start your can use your hand to help –
later the whip can be used to ask for the bow.
(Photos: Berit Seiboth)

Vocal commands

In this last step we introduce commands to initiate the trick. If you already give a command before starting the exercise – I use the term 'plié' – then that is the first additional step. In working through the exercise you have already undertaken a further step for introducing this command by tapping the horse on his chest with the hand holding the treat. Gradually replace your hand with the whip and touch him a bit further back every time so that eventually all you need to do is touch the horse under his stomach to call up the bow.

Finally, gradually reduce giving the horse his treat underneath his tummy by instead giving him a treat after he has performed the trick when he is standing up again. This process can take a long time and I would always recommend taking it slowly so that you don't discourage the horse.

forelegs. Put your hand between his forelegs and tap on the horse's chest a few times until the horse seeks a contact with your hand. Now move your hand back about a hand's breadth underneath his tummy sothat your horse lowers himself down and back over his quarters. The further back you bring the treat, the more the horse should shift himself down and back over his hindlegs. The forehand will be lowered towards the ground and the forelegs will be fully stretched out.

Be careful that your hand moves back and down, and only start moving your hand back once your horse has clearly shown that he has shifted his weight. The horse needs to precisely understand the sequence of movements for him to be able to quickly and successfully carry out a really spectacular bow.

It can take some time until the horse is able to perform a bow to this degree. Until then you should be satisfied with less, so as not to demand too much of your horse.

Checklist

Required skills for the bow

- Stretching exercises and feeding technique
- Moving the forelegs forwards
- Standing with the forelegs and hindlegs wide apart.

A question
of politeness

Now you have cast your first cautious glance into the world of the circus, you can take up your first challenge. The two-legged bow forms the basis for all other exercises performed in-hand. Building on this with a commitment to taking enjoyment from your work, you will easily reach the second level of circus training – kneeling.

The one-legged bow

For the one-legged bow the horse makes a backwards-downwards movement just as with the two-legged bow, but also bends one leg back so that he supports his weight on his cannon bone. You often see this movement being done in play fighting in the herd or when horses are stretching down to eat underneath a fence.

Just as with the two-legged bow, correct preparation is of key importance. Before starting, do some stretching exercises, stand correctly and run through the two-legged bow.

For the training itself you will require a whip and plenty of treats. Your horse should have a halter with a lead rope. If training in a fenced area, you could do without the lead rope.

If you and your horse have already mastered the two-legged bow, now teach him to lift his forelegs at the touch of the whip. I prefer touching the front of the cannon bone, since I want the horse to yield to the pressure exerted by the whip. Hold the whip as shown in the photo with the hand below the grip, so that at a later stage you can support the foreleg with the

Sandokan shows an exemplary one-legged bow

*C*hecklist

Required skills for the one-legged bow

- Stretching exercises and feeding technique
- Two-legged bow
- Park position

top of whip. If your horse doesn't respond to touching with the whip or doesn't lift his leg, you can lean on his shoulder so that he takes the weight off that leg. This will help the horse quickly learn to lift his leg in response to the whip. Practice lifting the forelegs and the touching aid with the whip in isolation before starting the bow so that you can draw on this once the horse is in position.

In addition touching the cannon bone with the whip is not only a prerequisite for the horse to be able to confidently perform the one-legged bow but is also important for kneeling.

Once you have successfully established the touching aid you can start with the real work for the one-legged bow. Stand the horse correctly. The hindlegs should be parallel and the forelegs, as with the two-legged bow, should be positioned forwards. Since the horse will need to balance himself on three legs, don't position the forelegs any wider than usual. Taking up the correct starting position is important so that your horse doesn't lose his balance when lowering himself down. If the hindlegs are too far under his stomach the horse will have to place even more weight on them than they already have to bear, and he won't have the space to set down his supporting leg. Hindlegs that are positioned too far back also won't help as the horse will then not be able to bow down enough.

Before starting the bow, improve your chances for success by positioning your horse correctly. (Photo: Berit Seiboth)

To start with, your horse needs to learn to lift his leg at the touch of the whip. (Photo: Berit Seiboth)

Both sides

Practice the one-legged bow on both sides to ensure that muscles develop evenly. Begin on your horse's (and your own!) best side. For kneeling it is important that the one-legged bow can be confidently performed on both sides. With some horses it takes months to go from starting out through to performing the one-legged bow independently. Don't get discouraged if at first you don't progress as quickly as you perhaps would like.

Giving the horse his treats when practicing the bow can prove to be a challenge for you and your horse's co-ordination. Make it easy for yourself by ensuring that the positioning of the feed and the way the horse lowers himself is perfected in the two-legged bow so that your horse knows where he needs to look for his treat. (Photo Berit Seiboth)

After putting the horse in position, touch the foreleg on which he should later support himself and hold onto the leg in the hand closest to the horse. Put your whip to one side and swap hands so that you now have that hand free to offer your horse his treats. Your horse should already be familiar with being offered treats on its chest from the two-legged bow training. Put your hand around the outside of the leg to its chest and indicate to your horse that there is a treat waiting for him. The next stage is a bit fiddly, as you then have to come in from behind with this hand while your horse is looking for his reward. Get your horse to 'lock on' to your hand as described in the previous chapter. It is important that you can control the horse in terms of speed and direction with this 'locking on' trick so the horse moves towards the ground slowly and in the correct position.

Now you are ready for the first attempt at the one-legged bow. Hold the bent leg gently in your hand, parallel to the ground, and move the feeding hand back underneath the horse's stomach so that the horse sinks back and down, just as with the other bow. The greatest challenge with this is keeping the feeding hand in position while bringing the bent leg down towards the ground. This is important, because if you offer the treat down too low the horse might end up doing a headstand, putting his forehead down on the ground, or he might try to bend the outstretched leg, which is going to interfere with his balance. If you get the feeling your horse is hard to hold then check the position of the bent leg. Typically you will have been holding the leg up for too long while he is trying to do what you are asking, or he will not be bent enough and so he will try to put the leg down.

Be careful that your horse doesn't put his carpal joint down first and that his foreleg stays vertical to the ground. A right angle between the cannon bone and foreleg is ideal for the horse to be able to support himself correctly.
(Photo Berit Seiboth)

Very obligingly, quite a few horses will carry out the movement at the first attempt and will lower themselves down so that the cannon bone rests on the ground. With horses that aren't too feed fixated, it may take a bit longer. If this is the case, give yourself time. If your horse has grasped what he is supposed to do then he will lower himself down until the leg is on the ground – even if just for short moment. At this point don't forget to tell him how brilliant he is. It is a good idea to offer lots of treats for as long as the horse stays down. This way he learns that it is worth remaining down. Once a horse has learned that he can grab a treat and then immediately jump up, it is difficult to correct.

As soon as your horse has grasped the exercise and is willing to lower himself down, you should begin to refine and correct his positioning. Take care to draw the bent leg back slowly, so that the tip of the hoof touches the ground first followed by the length of the cannon bone. The feeling of the ground is important for the horse's psyche, since later (when working more independently) he will need to find the right place to rest his leg himself. What you don't want is for the joint instead of the flat side of the cannon bone to support the horse's weight, because this will place unnessary stress on the joint and cause the horse considerable discomfort. To best support the horse's weight, the foreleg should ideally be at right angles to the ground. If the carpal joint is too far back thenthe horse can overbalance.

If the horse doesn't stretch his outstretched leg out fully or doesn't place his hoof flat on the ground, this is usually

To help changing from using your hand to the whip you can put the horse's leg on the whip as the horse lowers himself. At the start this requires some practice. It is important that the horse is encouraged to perform this exercise without the need for multiple commands. (Photos: Berit Seiboth)

because the muscles do not have sufficient elasticity, or the hindquarters are not sinking back enough so that the horse's weight is shifted too far forwards. You should also check the way in which you are offering the treats. Sometimes all you need to do is alter the position or speed to make a big difference.

Otherwise you will have to be patient until your horse has developed the right technique and his muscles can work in the right way.

Some horses with less than ideal proportions between their forelegs and length of head will often tend towards doing the previously mentioned headstand, even if they do everything correctly. To prevent this, change your technique and offer the treat in front of his chest, rather than lower down. Another common cause of the headstand is when the horse takes his weight onto the supporting leg badly. In this case he may have shifted his weight incorrectly and used his outstretched leg to keep his balance. What would have been more correct is for the horse to keep his balance by using his

head and outstretched leg, at the same time using the muscles in his stomach and hindquarters. This shows how important it is that the centre of gravity is pushed as far back as possible, which is only possible when the supporting leg lies fully flat on the ground.

Next of all, practice staying in position – this will be much easier if the horse's technique is correct. You need to have good timing and a well-trained eye. Don't try to stop your horse standing up but rather delay him from trying, by using feed. To begin with, give the horse as many treats as possible for as long as the horse stays down on the ground. Wait for the precise moment when your horse shows that he wants to get up and, before he does, give him the voice command to stand, such as 'up', and stand up straight yourself. Once your horse is really resting on his supporting leg then you could offer him some treats in front of his chest so the horse learns to hold his head up.

Once your horse has learned it is worth his while staying down, you can slowly extend the time between each treat and you

can start to stand up straighter until the point is reached when you will only need to give him a treat before ending the exercise.

At the same time you could also start to casually give the command for standing up. Simply say 'up' and energetically step forward to encourage your horse to stand up. Since your horse is likely to wait just in case there might be another treat, this should be quite easy. In addition, I use my whip placed on the top of the horse's leg as a sign the exercise is over.

As a last stage, move your horse from relying on aids from your hands to those given by your whip. The keener your horse is to do this exercise and the better the whip aids work, the simpler it will be to move from hand to whip. Instead of holding the horse's leg up, after touching the leg let it rest on the whip handle and continue to use your treats to get the horse to lower himself down. Check whether it is enough just to tap the horse underneath on his stomach to get him to lower his head. If your horse is looking for his treat and wants to lower himself, guide the leg back with the whip. Allow it to drop down early so that the tip of his hoof lands on the surface first and he can then seamlessly sink into the bow.

Often, when trying this, the horse will get stuck with the tip of his hoof in the surface as he tries to lower himself, resulting in the exercise being brought to a premature end. Here it is particularly important that the horse is encouraged to find his own solution and learn that he can slide his hoof over the surface. Help the horse out by either touch-

If you have done everything correctly, a touch with the whip should suffice for your horse to go down into the one-legged bow and stay there until he is given the command to stand up again. (Photo: Berit Seiboth)

ing his cannon bone or lifting the leg up a little. When the horse is performing the one-legged bow independently, it isn't important for him to hold the bent leg up the entire time but it is important that he lifts it up at the right moment and moves it back! What your horse needs at this phase of practicing is, above all, a sense of achievement.

Once this exercise has really sunk in you will not need to set it up correctly. Instead the horse will automatically take up the correct position and, once given the command, drop back onto his quarters.

You should also gradually reduce the use of treats. Start by only offering him treats when he is near the ground, once your horse has lowered himself down into position. Once he has fully understood this step, change to only feeding him after he has completed the trick and is squarely standing again. From this point on the horse will gradually carry out the exercise with more confidence, and once down, will stay there longer.

To get your horse used to the leg rope, put it on correctly and walk around together for a bit.

Patience and experience

Give your horse the time he needs to ultimately drop down into the full bow. Enjoy each individual step achieved that brings you closer to your goal. When using the leg rope, you need to reach a healthy medium between courage and caution. On the one hand, the horse should trust the rope as a support – this means you must not let go at every slight fidget. On the other hand, though, for safety's sake you must immediately release the rope if the horse should suddenly rear or kick out, which should never happen if you have prepared correctly. In this case, the only thing to do is to go back to the start, have plenty of patience and calmly try it all over again.

The one-legged bow with leg rope

As with nearly all exercises, there are a number of means to an end. In the last edi-

When working with the leg rope, the horse should wear a well-fitted headcollar and reins.

Firstly, get your horse to lift his leg when the whip is used to touch his cannon bone.
This later becomes the aid for the one-legged bow.

tion of my book I detailed the use of the leg rope, in which a rope placed over the horse's back replaced someone holding up the foreleg when asking the horse to move back into the one-legged bow. In the hands of an expert, the leg rope can be a kind and effective tool. I am reluctant to brand the leg rope in general as a means of force and I would also ask you not to judge it prematurely. Unfortunately, in practice, it is often misused to force a horse down on to the ground, either out of ignorance or lack of experience, or intentionally out of a belief that this is the correct method to use. I also class using it to prevent the horse standing back up as force, and this is irreconcilable with my philosophy.

A correctly fitted leg rope: It is important that the end is fed over the back and goes back through behind the forelegs and in front of the rope so that, when pulled, it doesn't slip back.

Working through the one-legged bow with leg rope

The horse lifts the leg held with the leg rope when the leg is touched with the tip of the whip. The horse is given a treat until he is used to being held in this position.

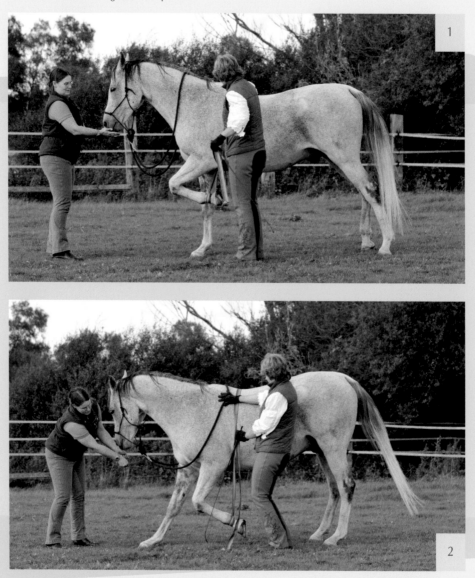

The right hand on the rope combined with the handler moving backwards provides the signal for the horse to go back. The leg rope is held with the left hand. At the first sign of any indication of a movement back you should stop, praise and go back to the starting position. Pay particular attention that you always take up pressure on the leg rope so that soon you won't need to use the reins at all.

Gradually your horse will trust himself to drop back lower and lower. Soon you shouldn't need the reins at all. If you like, continue to give the horse treats as he lowers himself down.

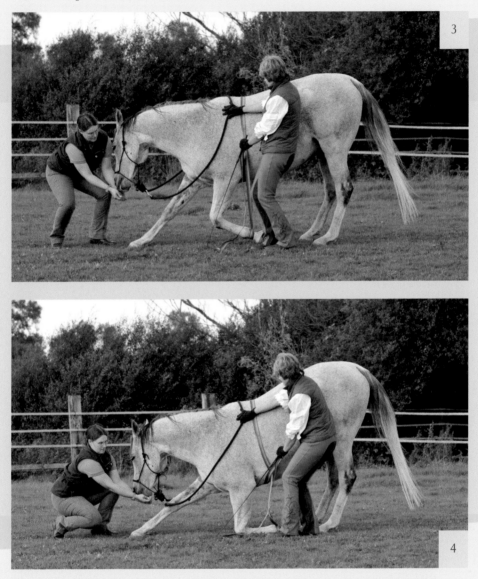

This is a perfect example: the cannon bone has been placed flat on the ground and his foreleg is at right angles. Praise and feed the horse as long as he maintains this position. As soon as you can feel that he wants to stand up, hold on to the leg rope briefly but firmly. If your horse reacts by remaining in place for even the briefest of time, praise him again. Loosen the rope then to allow the horse to stand, giving a clear command such as 'up'.

Once your horse can confidently drop down and stay down in the bow, ideally until you give him the command to stand up, you can start to reduce the use of the leg rope. Until this point the horse has understood that the command for the bow came from the leg rope. Now it is time to transfer over to the whip.

Take up the leg rope as usual, until your horse has lifted his leg. Hold on to the rope with the hand closest to the horse, where it crosses over near the horse's belly. With the whip in the other hand, touch the cannon bone with it. At the start use the leg rope (you shouldn't need the reins at all at this stage of training) to help with the backwards and down movement, and then gradually use the rope less until all you need is the whip command. The whip is then used as the 'stay' command on the horse's leg, as shown in the photos, until you give the command to stand up.

Next of all, use the leg rope direct from the foot to your hand (i.e. not looped around the horse's body). Touch the cannon bone with the whip and the rope should only come into play when necessary, lifting the horse's hoof slightly if required.

Finally, take the rope off entirely and give the command just by touching the horse's cannon bone. Congratulations on your perfect bow!

7

When used correctly, the leg rope can be just as much a kind method for training the bow.

The view that you can make a horse submissive by forcing him to the ground using a leg rope unfortunately persists. In fact, we should always treat our horses with respect and not offend their dignity by using such a forceful method. Such an abuse of our power can permanently damage the horse's mind and destroy his trust in humans, quite apart from the risk of injury to both the horse and trainer.

If you should decide to use the leg rope, I would always recommend that you find a competent instructor in your area who can support both you and your horse on a regular basis and help you solve any problems that arise. This is particularly important if you are inexperienced in either circus or in-hand work.

After years of practice and many courses later, I have refined my technique to such an extent that I need to use a leg rope only in very rare cases. There are so many ways that you can use to encourage and motivate a horse, and in most cases I find the use of the leg rope to be unnecessary and outdated. There is also therisk that, without professional help, the inexperienced handler won't cope and as a result, the horse suffers. This is one reason why, in this edition, I am not giving a detailed description of this technique. Instead I hope I am able to show you the way to achieve the one-legged bow through a systematic and targeted set of exercises without the need for a leg rope.

Firstly, give the aids for the bow as usual from the ground whilethe rider sits still, so that the horse can get used to the additional weight and learns to balance himself.

Later, you will be able to give the touching aids from above.

The ridden one-legged bow

Now your horse can perform the one-legged bow on both sides smoothly and correctly, you can progress to trying it with a rider. There are no real benefits for the horse in terms of added suppleness, but it is naturally much harder and more strenuous for the horse to balance and carry the rider's weight in addition to his own. If possible, use a rider who is as light as possible especially when starting to teach this exercise. This means you can continue to give the familiar aids from the ground. Once your horse isused to the additional weight, equip the rider with a long whip so the aids can be given from above. It is unlikely the rider will be able to reach the same spot that the

horse is used to being given the aids on when you have been on the ground. Most horses quickly grasp which exercise they are being asked to perform. Get the rider to touch the cannon bone on the side while you give the voice command for the one-legged bow. The rider should try not to lean too far forwards or to the side, in case this throws the horse out of balance. You should be there just in case you are needed to reinforce the aids, but only step in if necessary. That way, your horse should quickly understand that he should perform the bow when ridden. Next, you can get into the saddle yourself and you should soon be able to perform the bow without any further help. Don't overdo this exercise, however, as it is physically very demanding for the horse.

The kneel in twin pack – almost circus ready!

Kneeling

You have now laid the foundation stone for further work with the one-legged bow. The next step in the scale of training for circus work is kneeling. When kneeling, the horse bends both forelegs and drops down onto his cannon bones. This is the last phase in the sequence of actions when a horse spontaneously lies down, and also the last step when you are teaching him to lie down on command.

There are essentially two ways to achieve kneeling: either you work on the kneel from the one-legged bow, or you try to try to get the horse to kneel by touching both forelegs at the same time when he is standing. In the case of version one, you usually achieve good results in a reasonable time as long as you have conscientiously and carefully taught your horse to perform the one-legged bow. Version two is by no means suitable for all horses, but works especially well with sensitive horses. Sometimes, however, you will realise that this method is not suitable after all and have to change to the other method, so you will need to consider carefully whether the horse is suitable for this second version.

When kneeling, the hindquarters and stomach muscles bear most of the weight. Only then can the forelegs bend.

Required skills and preparation

Kneeling places great physical and mental demands on a horse. When kneeling, the horse gives up the majority of his ability to flee, since he can't jump up and take flight quickly from this position. As with all other exercises requiring the horse to drop down onto the ground, it is a great sign of trust when the horse kneels.

Since kneeling is an extension of the one-legged bow, the horse should be able to perform this on both sides on command and he should be happy to remain in the bow for some time. Once kneeling, you don't have much opportunity to correct the way a horse is positioned. A horse that is not confident in the one-legged bow will have problems with the kneel. If the kneel absolutely doesn't work then go back and work on the one-legged bow.

The kneel is physically much more strenuous than the one-legged bow. The hindquarters and the stomach bear the majority of the horse's weight. When kneeling, the back half of the horse is responsible for

ensuring the horse can maintain the mobility of the forehand in order to bend his front legs. In the second training method, with the horse at halt, the hindquarters will for a brief moment – bear the horse's entire weight. Also, when standing back up, it is only when the quarters take the horse's weight that he is able to jump up on to his forelegs and stand up. Once kneeling, the neck and head are held up – meaning the muscles in the neck and shoulder have to remain tensed. You can often tell how well-suited horses are for learning the kneel by watching them play and fight – especially in the case of stallions and other playful horses. A horse that fluidly drops into a kneel when playing in the field will learn to kneel on command much faster than one that avoids kneeling at all costs or opts instead to go into a one-legged bow to evade an attacker. This is often the case with big or heavy horses.

*C*hecklist

Required skills for kneeling from the one-legged bow:

- An accomplished one-legged bow on both sides
- Acceptance of the touching aid on the forelegs
- Ability to bear sufficient weight through his quarters in the bow

Developing the kneeling from the one-legged bow

To further develop kneeling out of the one-legged bow doesn't require any special knack from the horse and is usually fairly easy to achieve. In preparation, first of all, practice doing the one-legged bow alternatively on each side in quick succession. Ask your horse to stay down in the bow for a brief time and then ask him to stand again. By going from one side to the other, it will make your horse more sensitive to the touching aid that is require for the kneel.

By strictly separating the one-legged bow to the left and to the right, as is the case up until now, the horse has learnt to distinguish between the touching aid on the left and the right. Now he needs to learn a more fluid application of the aids, which in time combines the one-legged bow on the right and the left into one movement. You should allow plenty of time to practice this so that the horse achieves the required levels of skill and strength.

Kneeling from the one-legged bow. Firstly, give the aids that are already familiar from the one-legged bow.

Pay attention that your horse is bearing enough weight on the supporting bent, leg, and that the hindquarters are sufficiently underneath him to ensure that the outside shoulder remains as free as possible. The one-legged bow can in this case be a bit backwards.

With the correct preparation, your horse should soon respond by bending his outstretched leg if you touch him on the spot where you ask for the bow.

And there you have the kneel.

As a rough estimate, six alternative one-legged bows (three per side) should suffice. Watch out for any signs of tiredness in your horse and, if necessary, cut this back. On no account should you overdo it, and remember to praise your horse for every correct step carried out so as not to spoil what will be a strenuous exercise for him. The entire process should ideally have something fun and playful about it.

There will be some clever horses that, even at this stage, show the first signs of kneeling. If this happens you should try to build on any of these attempts – but don't get too fixated on this happening. If this method shows no clear success after a few attempts (in other words, no signs of both forelegs lifting as if to kneel) then go back to the normal series of movements and give your horse the time needed to learn how to kneel.

Once the horse is sensitised to the touching aid, ask him to perform the one-legged bow. Some horses find kneeling from this movement easier if you ask for it on their better side. It might, however, work out better on the horse's 'worse' side since he will find it easier to bend the leg back (which will be the one on his better side).

Until now the leg has been outstretched, but we are now trying to get the horse to bend the leg back in order to show those first signs of kneeling. To achieve this, you need to give the aid for the opposite one-legged bow during the bow itself. Ideally, you should quickly (but quietly) change sides so you can give the aid from the 'correct' side. Alternatively, you can try to reach across and touch the outstretched leg, or failing

this ask someone else for help. Most horses will be quick to understand what you are asking and will try to at least move the outstretched leg back. At this stage, you should immediately praise the smallest of attempts. Of course, it is fantastic if the first attempt ends in the horse kneeling – but do not rely on this happening and potentially miss the opportunity to offer praise at precisely the right time. This could have negative repercussions later.

Initially you should reward any hint of the outstretched leg bending. Be exaggerated in your praise – your enthusiasm will carry over to your horse and it will not be long before the horse shows his first, even brief, tentative signs of kneeling.

At this stage of training it will become clear whether the one-legged bow has been taught correctly. A horse that does not support himself on a bent leg that is at right angles to the ground, and as a result tips his weight too far forward or back, will find it considerably harder to maintain his balance and show the necessary strength that kneeling requires.

Even if they try, most horses can only muster up the strength to keep kneeling if the supporting leg is as straight as a pillar. This must be learnt in the one-legged bow.

Training the horse to kneel from standing

The second variation utilises the horse's natural playing and fighting behaviour. It is particularly suitable for stallions and youngsters, since these tendencies are usu-

ally more highly developed in such horses. You will, of course, find mares and geldings that can learn to kneel using this method, providing they possess the necessary degree of sensitivity. By clever use of the whip on the cannon bone, to replicate an opponent nipping his forelegs, the horse should pull his legs back. If you would like to teach your horse to kneel without firstly teaching him the one-legged bow, you could also try this variation. However, I recommend that you follow the training sequence previously described, starting with the one-legged bow.

Position yourself in front of your horse at an angle, holding him by his lead rope, or have a helper hold the horse for you. Touch him on the front of one of his cannon bones. If your horse is familiar with the one-legged bow and with the use of the whip, he should respond by lifting and bending up his foreleg. If your horse has not yet mastered the one-legged bow, you will have to first teach him this movement. To do this, tap his cannon bone for as

long as it takes for him to react. It is irrelevant how strongly he reacts – the main thing is that he reacts at all. Basically, it is better to annoy and nag at the horse until he responds instead of increasing the intensity of the aid, which will only cause the horse to get cross.

The correct reaction would be for him to quickly fold back his leg. Sensitise the

For playful horses, especially youngsters and stallions, you can try to train the horse to kneel by using the whip to imitate the game played by herd members when they try to bite each other's front legs. This will cause the horse to lift his legs.

horse to this aid and ask him to lift up alternative legs, doing so in quicker and quicker succession. Ideally, the horse should set his legs back down slightly under his centre of gravity and shift his weight slightly forwards. In between times, ask the horse to take one or two steps forwards. He should stretch out his head and neck forwards and down since then the horse is more likely to think of lifting both forelegs up at the same time.

Give plenty of praise whenever the time between changing legs is reduced. If the horse then takes more weight back on to his quarters or lifts both forelegs at the same time, this is exactly the response you are looking for. You should be really pleased and praise the horse immediately. You can now build on this step until the horse touches the ground with both cannon bones for the first time.

With this method, you don't have any opportunity to correct the horse's outline. This is why, in some circumstances, it will take longer for the horse to understand the ins and outs of the leg technique required for kneeling. Additionally, asI have already mentioned, this method is not suitable for every horse. If there is no real progress over a short time it is probably best to try the other method.

Maintaining the kneel and standing up again

Once the horse has understood that he should rest with both cannon bones on the ground for a moment, he then has to learn to extend the length of time for which he is kneeling. If the horse remains kneeling of his own accord, great! All you thenneed to do is to gradually delay giving him praise and, as you have from the start, establish a clear command for him to stand up again.

Many horses will jump up again as soon as their cannon bones touch the ground. The first step would be to reinforce the precise moment when they touch the ground so the horse understands that this action was correct and what you wanted him to do. You have already practiced patience when working on the one-legged bow – it is no different here. It usually takes some time until the horse is happy to maintain the kneeling position.

Once this happens, it is important to reward the horse when kneeling and start to work on the command to end the exercise and for him to stand up again. To do this, stand at an angle to the front of the horse, looking at his head. Hold the whip in the hand closest to the horse. If the horse is kneeling, hold the whip in front of the horse's foreleg and touch him quietly on that leg. Before the horse stands up of his own accord, turn to the front swinging with the whip and say 'up' with vigour and energy.

Here the whip is used as a 'stop' sign, so taking it away – together with your voice command – are the signals for the horse to stand up. Praise then follows as he gets to his feet and also when the horse is standing up. It isn't important whether the horse stands up one leg at a time or jumps up with both legs at the same time, which is what most horses will do over time.

When kneeling, just as in the one-legged bow, your horse should also learn to understand the use of the whip on his foreleg as a stop sign.

Kneeling when ridden

If your horse has learnt to kneel and can remain in position until he is given the command to stand up, you have achieved a great deal. A horse finds it very tiring to kneel so don't ask for too much and, even when he is more experienced, you should really only ask him to do it a few times in succession.

You can also ask the horse to kneel when ridden – but consider whether you are doing the horse any favours. Only a few horses have the ability and the strength to kneel correctly with a rider on board. Most find this hard, especially standing up afterwards. You would be better to confine yourself to riding the one-legged bow, which looks more graceful and has more value in terms of suppleness.

$\mathcal{T}$rustingly
to the ground

Having a horse that will lie trustingly next to you, possibly even lying flat out on his side, can be one of a horse owner's highpoints in life. If you have worked through the circus scales of training, through the two-legged and one-legged bow and the kneel, then your horse is ideally prepared for lying down on command. But as we all know, there are many roads that lead to Rome – this applies in particular to lying down.

Lying down upright

Lying down upright, with his head and neck off the ground and his legs tucked underneath him, is the typical resting position for horses. The way to get to this position varies from horse to horse, and different methods are possible. If your horse enjoys rolling and is happy to do it in your pres-

ence, you could put this to use and teach him to lie down from rolling. But the classical method of training the horse to lie down is from kneeling or from the one-legged bow.

Required skills and preparation

Seen from a physical and mental standpoint, lying down is a very demanding exercise. On a psychological level, in particular, there is no other exercise that strengthens and tests the trust forged between you and your horse quite so much. Besides improving the horse's suppleness, the aim of this exercise should be to cement or gain your horse's full trust – and under no circumstances should it be used to as a demonstration of dominance. The true benefits of this exercise will really only be felt when it can be done with the horse's full co-operation.

Lying down is great for developing suppleness, but is particularly good for strengthening trust between horse and handler.

Does your horse remain lying down when you enter his stable while he is taking a nap or when you go out to him in the paddock? If you can answer yes, this is a good sign that your horse will be mentally prepared for this exercise. When starting to train this movement, it is essential that the right conditions are in place. Start only when you are absolutely sure that the horse is on good form and that you will be undisturbed.

If there is somewhere where your horse likes to roll and it is a safe area to train in, then use this. Obviously it needs to have a soft and even surface. If you have someone to help you, this person should also be well known to and trusted by your

$\mathcal{C}$hecklist

Required skills for lying down

- Sufficient trust
- Proficiency in kneeling or the one-legged bow
- Ideally, competence in performing the mountain goat exercise
- Ability to bend the neck to both sides

horse, so that they don't unintentionally become a disturbing factor instead.

The horse's natural behaviour would be to rest when in the lying down upright position. Body and soul can relax and recuperate, but the horse remains in a position from which he can quickly stand up by stretching out both front legs and (if necessary) take flight. To lie down, the horse bends front and back legs almost simultaneously and takes up a kneeling position for a short moment, before sinking down and placing his legs sideways underneath his body. Taking up this position is strenuous and most of the horse's body weight is carried through his hindquarters and the rear part of his stomach.

The best way of training your horse to lie down on command is best established by observing his natural behaviour. Most horses will lie down by kneeling, but others will lie down via the one-legged bow. You should take this into account when working out your sequence of movements. In the case of horses that avoid kneeling down when playing with others in the herd, using the one-legged kneel may prove to be the easiest route to success with this exercise.

Even with relatively little experience and providing there is sufficient mutual trust a horse can be taught to lie down using his desire to roll.

Teaching the horse to lie down from the roll

This somewhat unconventional method can be very effective with some horses, and is suitable for young or inexperienced horses since little previous training is required. Unfortunately, many trainers insist you can't train a horse to lie down on command using this method. I, on the other hand, know of countless horses that have learnt to lie down this way.

In any case, this approach requires a deep and intense relationship between the

If you praise your horse for as long as he is lying down, he will soon understand that lying down is what you wanted him to do.

horse and his trainer. Unlike the other two methods this relationship cannot be developed during the training itself but must be present from the start.

The prerequisite for this variation is that the horse enjoys rolling (in your presence as well as at other times) and you know his rolling habits, such as when and where this happens. Many stabled horses use any opportunity to roll once they are out of their box, particularly when they have the opportunity to roll on sand. They will also probably enjoy rolling after they have been ridden.

This approach consists of prompting this behaviour as often as possible. As soon as you can, you should hold the horse by his lead rope while he rolls, without interfering with his movement. Initially, you will need to keep some distance from the horse.

Gradually, try to get closer to the horse's head. Once your horse isn't bothered by your presence, offer him some treats on your outstretched hand. Don't be discouraged if your horse isn't interested, just keep trying. At some stage, your horse will notice the feed being offered to him and

be delighted at the unexpected snack. Give him plenty of treats for as long as he stays lying down. Stop feeding him the instant he starts trying to stand up.

When you have done this several times in succession, it shouldn't take long until your horse expects a treat before he stands up. That is fantastic. You should be really pleased and offer your horse plenty of praise as well as treats. In the next step, your horse may interrupt his rolling or possibly not even start to roll as soon as you offer him treats. Gradually, you can narrow down the distance between you until you are actually touching the horse. Don't underestimate the time it takes until the horse allows himself to be stroked when lying down and, above all, don't get frustrated when it doesn't work straight away. At some stage it will work and from then on it won't take long until the horse will lie down on command.

For this stage it is necessary for you to establish a command for lying down. A voice command such as 'Lie down' has worked for me, together with tapping the whip on the ground. Your posture and gaze should also be directed towards the ground. Give your command and the associated signal at the same time as the horse lies down. This will gradually condition the horse to your aids and it will become the signal to lie down.

Using rolling to train the horse to lie down can take considerably longer than other more conventional methods. You cannot rule out the possibility that your horse won't actually lie down using this method. If this is the case, you will need to use the following methods using the one-legged bow or kneeling, which considering the benefits for suppleness, is an advantage. In addition, you will then be able to determine the side on which your horse lies down and be able to train both sides evenly.

Lying down from the kneel

According to the scales of circus training, the classical method for teaching a horse to lie down is through kneeling and (ideally) with the help of the mountain goat exercise. Fit your horse with his headcollar and reins, and find a suitable spot with soft ground. Position yourself so you will be standing with the horse's back to you once he is lying down. Practice bending the horse's head and neck away from you. Take up a light pull on the outside rein, until the horse turns his head away from you and then praise him. If your horse is familiar with the warm-up and stretching exercises from the introductory chapter, he should not find it hard to carry out this sequence of movements.

Now ask your horse to kneel as usual. Stretch over his back and take up the outside rein and ask him to bend his head as we have just practiced. This should cause the horse to lie down with his back to you. If your horse is small enough you can make it a bit easier by using a carrot to tempt him to bend round and then feed him over the top of his back until he lies down.

It is recommended for all horses, as with the mountain goat exercise, that you ask

To get from kneeling to lying down, ask your horse to bend his neck using the outside rein.

the horse to move his hindlegs well underneath himself until he naturally lies down through the shoulder closest to you. If this doesn't work, or if your horse can't do the mountain goat exercise, then you can give a gentle pull on the reins and bring the horse's shoulder closer to the ground until he lies down. Under no circumstances should you try to 'throw' your horse over by bending his head so far round that he loses his balance. The bending of the neck should simply act as something to make him start thinking about what it is that you want. Sometimes it can help if you keep the horse in the kneel for a while and then ask the horse to bend his neck again and ask him to lie down afresh. Let time work for you until the horse has

understood what he should do and lies down.

Once you have mastered this step, introduce a new aid into the process. Touch the horse's cannon bone when kneeling, while you give the usual aids for lying down, and give a carefully-selected voice command. From now on you should always use this voice command to ask for this exercise. Stop giving the aid once the horse has laid down – and enjoy your success!

Most horses can quickly differentiate between when you are asking them to kneel and when to lie down. Despite this, it might be that your horse will lie down when you are actually asking him to do something else. This is usually only a temporary problem. Ignore this incorrect behaviour, ask

Trustingly
to the ground

An experienced horse lying down. The horse drops his quarters and transfers his weight back.

Touching his quarters with the whip causes him to step more underneath himself.

Lying down is the logical result.

your horse to stand up again, and just try again. Make sure there are real and clear differences in the aids you give and try to be very targeted and controlled in the way you give them.

With time, the need for you to influence the sequence of movements your horse makes will reduce, and lying down will become more fluent and look more natural – becoming more like the way a horse would lie down in his natural environment.

Allow your horse to develop his own technique, as long as you get the result you want.

Lying down from the one-legged bow

Should your horse find kneeling difficult for physical reasons, or has not yet learnt how to kneel, you can also teach him to lie down from the one-legged bow. The

When lying down via the one-legged bow, the horse will roll over his outstretched leg onto his outside shoulder. You need to lead his head around to you.
(Photo: Gabi Appelt)

disadvantage of this method is that you are closer to the horse's hooves, since you need to turn the horses head towards you and the horse then lies down with his legs stretched out towards you. For this reason you should be particularly careful when using this method to teach your horse to lie down.

Ask your horse to go into the one-legged bow as usual, and draw the horse's head round towards you with either the reins or treats. Practice this until, hopefully, the horse lies down through his outside shoulder.

If this doesn't work, straighten the horse again and ask him to shift his balance out and back over his quarters. You might recognise this 'swaying' exercise from the preparation for the one-legged bow, as the aids stem from this movement. These may be a tug on the reins, or a hand placed on the horse's point of shoulder to gently

Be sure to keep at a safe distance since the horse's legs will be on your side when he lies down from the one-legged bow.
(Photo: Gabi Appelt)

push him backwards. Whilst we want to avoid the horse dropping his chest in the one-legged bow, here this is exactly what we are trying to cause. The further the horse transfers his weight back, the closer his chest will become to the ground and the greater will be the bend through his hocks. Praise the horse at every moment at which he gets closer to the ground. The closer he gets to the ground, the more he will be prepared to lower himself down. You can also use the mountain goat exercise to ask him to move his hindlegs more under his centre of gravity, which in turn will cause him to lie down.

When doing the swaying exercise, your horse will probably drop down of his own accord at some stage. If not, hold on to the outside rein and ask for more bend, to give him more of an idea that you want him to lie down, and give him time until he is ready to do this of his own accord.

Once your horse has learned the exercise and the command linked with it, soon he won't fully stretch out that leg but rather keep it slightly bent. He may even (of his own accord) bend both front legs and kneel before he lies down, because he will have realised this is more comfortable, or he may have made the connection to the way he normally lies down. It is not unusual that a horse develops his own technique for moving from the one-legged bow into lying down. Let him have the freedom to do this, as long as the result is correct.

A frequent problem experienced when a horse learns to lie down via the one-legged bow is that the outstretched leg stays stretched out. Sometimes this sorts itself out over time and, if not, there is no other way than to try to teach him to lie down from kneeling. The easier solution is to train this exercise from the kneel. With most horses that know how to lie down from both the one-legged bow and the kneel, combining both is never any great problem.

To encourage the horse to stay down, give him lots of treats and teach him the command for standing up.

Staying down

In the final step you need to teach your horse to stay lying down for a longer time. This doesn't usually cause any great problems. Once lying down, tweak the reins so the horse turns his head around towards his stomach, and feed him. Start by reaching over his back to give him the treats. This means the horse's neck will remain bent and he won't be able to jump up as quickly. In addition, this technique will come in useful when you are teaching your horse to lie down flat.

Don't feed your horse for too long, otherwise he may jump up before you have asked him to. He should learn to stand up only once you have given him the appropriate command. To get the horse to stand up, give him the same command that you have already established in the one-legged bow and kneel. If this doesn't work, you can also use the rope to encourage him to stand.

As a final polish, you can work on the horse's head carriage. Until now you have given him treats across his back. Now go to the other side and gradually move your position forwards, until the horse is holding his head straight and in a more natural position over his chest.

Lying down flat – a real sign of trust

Lying down flat is a special type of lying down and not every horse has enough innate trust to do this and stay there in this position. But this is, if nothing else, a question of training.

In a horse's natural pattern of behaviour, he will only lie down flat in this defence-less position when he is in deep sleep. He lies on his side and stretches all four legs out – it is a break not just for his body but for all of his senses. The horse trusts the herd leader will protect him and let him know if there is danger approaching. If this were not the case in the wild, he would be doomed because from this position he wouldn't be able to get up and flee in time if a predator were to attack. This also explains why the horse must not only have particularly great trust in you, but also accept you as his herd leader.

You should stand behind your horse once he is lying down, with the legs pointing away from you. Using the reins, ask your horse to turn his head towards his stomach. Try to turn the head sufficiently towards you so that he eventually lies down flat. Watch that the inside rein (the one on the inside bend) is lying against the neck, since later that will be the signal for him to lie down flat. You should also introduce a voice command, for example 'flat'. Don't forget to reward even the smallest of responses, since this exercise isn't exactly child's play. You can also try to feed the

Unconditional trust is essential for your horse to
be prepared to lie flat out.

Checklist

horse over his back, as you did at the initial
stages of teaching him to stay lying down.
Offer him the treat further and further
back across his back, so that he is encouraged to lie down.

At first, most horses will either try to
immediately get up again or at least sit
up. Don't stop him doing this but rather
allow your horse the freedom to decide

Required skills for lying
flat out

- Sitting upright
- Bending the neck on both sides

89

what feels comfortable. Keep practicing and try to always give your horse plenty of praise when he is lying down.

When your horse does eventually stay down, don't draw it out for too long, but rather try to give the command for the horse to sit back up before he wants to himself. To do this, walk in front of your horse or move to the other side and give the usual voice command as well as using treats to entice him back up into an upright, lying position. Depending on the horse, you could ask him to lie back down or stand up to end the exercise, and then repeat it later.

When your horse has understood that you want him to lie flat on the ground, you can start to differentiate the way you

By skilfully offering your horse treats over his back, he is encouraged to lie down flat.

Continue to offer treats for as long as the horse is lying down and ask him to stand up before he does it of his own accord.

give the aids. Instead of the reins, use your hand to gently press against the neck while you give the voice command for lying down. Later, you could use the whip handle on the neck instead of your hand so you don't have to bend down to your horse. And voilà! Your horse is now lying at your feet. Enjoy this intimate moment of togetherness and the deep connection that binds you both.

$\mathscr{P}$lease
take your seat

Now it is time to expand your repertoire with another exciting circus trick: sitting. Despite the high level of suppleness this demands, once they understand what they have to do horses seem to really enjoy this exercise. In addition, audiences always seem to be fascinated by a horse that is sitting up, perhaps apart from anything else because of the charm and self-confidence horses seem to exude when doing this.

Required skills and preparation

Sitting is actually part of the process of standing up when a horse has been lying down. The horse stretches one or both forelegs out in front of it, shifts his weight forwards while bringing his hindlegs underneath himself to push energetically upwards to a standing position. Often the horse will swing his head and neck to create additional momentum. Since this extra momentum is then lacking when he stands up out of the sit, this exercise requires particularly great effort. It also requires a great amount of co-ordination and physical awareness from the horse. since the slow, controlled movement that this exercise requires is usually totally new to the horse. In this circus version of sitting, the horse pushes himself up with his forelegs and steps around a few steps around his quarters so that the forelegs are positioned approximately in front of or in the middle of his hindlegs. He then stays in this sitting position. Sitting is really an artificial position, although it does have its roots in the range of a horse's natural behaviour.

While the horse is sitting, his entire top line is being stretched, in particular the muscles in his chest and shoulders. The muscles in his hindquarters are almost entirely relaxed. Depending on how upright

Ponies often find sitting easier than horses do.

the horse is sitting, the hip joints and the lumbar part of the spine will be put under stress, which is why this exercise should not be taught to horses with problems in these areas. The greatest strain occurs when the horse is standing up. This strain is especially strong on the hocks and knees. You should be particularly careful with horses that have had injuries or health problems in these areas, and it is recommended that you consult your vet before starting.

The condition of the surface you are working on for this exercise is even more important than it has been for the work until now. It should be soft but firm enough to offer sufficient grip, so the horse's hooves don't slip when he pushes himself up. If not, this can quickly lead to frustration and it could make it more difficult for you later to enthuse the horse for this exercise. Test the surface yourself by digging your heel into the surface with your toes pointing up, and push. If your foot slips, your horse is likely to do the same. Sometimes all you have to do is water the surface and let it dry a bit. Otherwise, working in a paddock is fine, as long as your horse isn't distracted too much by the grass.

Your horse should now be able to lie down upright and flat on command, and be able to switch between the two versions with no problems. The Spanish walk can also come in useful (refer page 103), as your horse is already familiar with the aids for stretching out the forelegs. What is absolutely essential is that your horse halts and backs up on command.

Always remember to warm your horse up properly before beginning every training session. Ask him for several of the circus tricks that have already been learned, particularly the change from lying upright to flat.

Stretching the forelegs

The first phase of sitting is stretching out the forelegs from the lying position. You must ensure your horse stretches out both legs without then jumping up. From the upright position, carefully touch the front leg closest to you and observe whether your horse moves his leg. If your horse doesn't react, try different places on the leg and (if necessary) be a little firmer with your touch. As soon as your horse reacts, even with the slightest twitch of the leg, reward him immediately. That is the start of a stretch. If your horse is familiar with the Spanish walk, he will probably reward your efforts quite quickly with an outstretched leg. If you really don't progress any further then you will have to pull the leg forward by hand. Take hold of the leg just above the hoof and move it forward, following the curve of the horse's natural movement, to place it on the ground in front. Stay in this position for a moment and give your horse treats. Ask him to lie down again, step back and only then ask him to stand up. Practice this sequence several times and only start on the second leg when your horse is happy to maintain his position with one outstretched leg.

The method for the second leg is exactly the same, with you praising even the smallest of correct moves. Even if it works with the first leg, this doesn't mean it will work just as well with the second. Once your horse has stretched out the second leg, remain briefly in this position and then ask the horse to lie down flat again, step back and ask him to stand up.

Repeat this exercise until your horse no longer tries to jump up. At the start, jumping up is a normal reaction since your horse doesn't yet know what you want from him. To avoid this situation, whilst your horse is happy to stay in the desired position, don't extend this period for too long but

*C*hecklist

Required skills for sitting

- Lying down upright
- Lying flat
- Possible Spanish walk
- Halt
- Backing up

By offering plenty of treats once the horse is sitting with his legs stretched out, you will delay the horse standing up. (Photo: Gabi Appelt)

instead only very gradually lengthen this time. Offer treats so the head and neck are straight and at a point around the height of the middle of the point of the shoulder. Feeding closer to the ground is also beneficial. Before your horse can even think about standing up, ask him to lie back down. After several attempts, you will be able to use lying down to prevent the horse standing up.

Sitting up

The moment has now arrived for you to begin the actual sitting up exercise. You will have to experiment to find out which of the various techniques is right for your horse.

Firstly, try the following method. Put your hand on your horse's chest, press lightly and ask your horse to back up. If your horse starts to push himself up, praise and reward him. Give the treats as high up and as close to the chest as possible. This will make the horse arch his neck, which further encourages him to push himself up. For some horses, this type of feeding can be enough to get them to push themselves up into the sit.

If this doesn't work, ask a helper to feed your horse while you carefully ask the

The horse pushes himself up with the hindlegs and then 'steps' around his quarters until he is eventually sitting up.

horse to back up with wide reins. Be generous with the treats. If you reward any sign of movement backwards, your horse will get more and more confident and push himself up more and more. If your horse slips as he is pushing himself up or if he lies down again, ask him to lie down flat and start over again. This helps you to put the different parts of the exercise clearly into context for him.

At the start, your horse will find the action of pushing himself up quite hard. On the other hand, to remain sitting and then stand up requires more strength, and the closer the chest is to the ground, the fewer steps back your horse has made. The higher he sits up, the easier he will find it. Once the penny has dropped, he will sit up as much as he can. Most horses enjoy this position so it isn't hard, with the encouragement of praise and treats, to get him to stay like this for a few seconds if not longer.

Standing up

This part of the exercise is easy. Simply step back and ask your horse to stand up using the usual command. Standing up from the sit requires a huge amount of effort from both the forehand and hindquarters. The horse leans forwards over the forehand as far as possible, and then pushes up through the quarters. The sequence of movements is similar to standing up from lying down, although the horse can't swing himself up and use the momentum as he does when standing up from lying down. Don't be surprised if the horse has to find his balance and sways a bit. This sequence is new to him and requires practice to coordinate everything. It may take a bit of time until the horse has enough strength to smoothly stand up, so practice this exercise regularly but not too often.

Standing from sitting, especially out of a tall sitting position, places great demands on a horse's co-ordination and strength.
(Photo: Gabi Appelt)

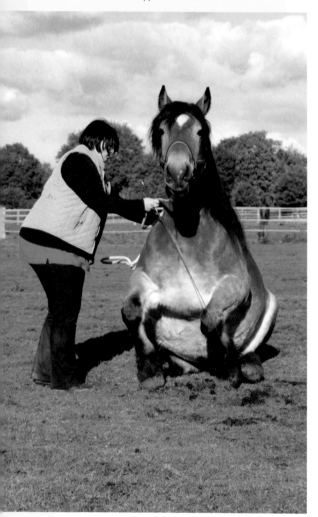

Sitting up tall

Your horse has now learned to push himself upright out of his recumbent position, and to stay there. In the next stage, he has to learn to walk around his quarters with his front legs, so his forelegs come to rest in the centre and in front of his hindlegs. This means the horse is straight and not tilted on to one of his hindquarters.

Use a carrot to tempt your horse around into the desired position. Reward every step at first, and later you can reduce the frequency and give the horse his reward when he has completed the movement. If this doesn't work, ask a helper to feed him while you give him the aids for turning with the reins. Use this opportunity to establish a command using the whip for this 'walking round'. Touch the outside shoulder in addition to giving him a feed reward, so he moves away from the pressure. Later on, touching him with the whip should suffice and once the horse has understood what it is you want, he will at some stage of his

Sitting up tall: the forelegs are positioned centrally, the horse is upright with his weight placed evening across the hindquarters, and the spine is straight. (Photo: Gabi Appelt)

own accord move his forelegs around into this central position.

To shape the horse's sit even more, once the horse is sitting centrally, you could try to get him to sit up even taller. The horse's build will determine how upright he will be able to sit. Horses with short legs and straight backs can usually sit up taller. However, this is also a question of training.

Standing up out of this tall sitting position demands even more effort from the horse than before, especially from his hindlegs. The horse pushes himself up into a position similar to that assumed for the mountain goat exercise, and places his legs into a more relaxed position.

Lying down from sitting

Whatever happens, you really should teach your horse to lie down from sitting. It is not only a good lesson in obedience, but also an excellent exercise for suppleness. Since this sequence of movements is not part of a horse's natural repertoire, you will need to be particularly careful and conscientious when training.

Once sitting, give your horse some treats low down between his forelegs and encourage him gradually forwards, so he slowly slips downwards. At first your horse will be puzzled, since you are now asking for something you were initially trying to prevent. Some horses are absolutely determined not to lie down. They seem to be saying 'Look how clever I am, I don't fall down'. If your horse is like this, it's not wrong of him, so you will need to take plenty of time and keep on trying.

As soon as your horse has sunk down, ask him to lie down flat for a moment and then ask him to lie upright. From this up-right position, ask your horse to stand up again. Repeat this sequence of movements again and again (not on the same day!) and then begin to touch the back of the front legs when you are feeding him. Once your horse has understood that you want him to end up lying down in the upright position, he will start to move his forelegs. Give him lots of praise and it won't be long until he stops slipping down from the sit, but will instead bend his forelegs and lie down in a more correct manner.

More than 'just' sitting

You should only ever consider riding a horse into the sitting position – if at all = after long and thorough training, and only then with a horse that finds it easy to stand up again. The strain in standing up without a rider is already great enough; the risk

Pure suppleness

Sitting is a real exercise in suppleness – providing you practice it as soon as possible from both sides. It is normal that, when sitting, a horse has a better side – however, you should always try to work both sides the same.

Once your horse can sit down from both sides, you can do a real workout: ask your horse into a tall sit, stay there, and then encourage him to continue to 'walk' around his hindquarters. At the 'pivot point' he will have to reposition himself and then, after a few more steps, you can ask him to lie down on the other side. The trainer, Eva Wiemers, very appropriately calls this a 'seated pirouette'.

Sitting is a good exercise to combine with others, such as the Spanish greeting

of injury with the addition of a rider's weight should not be underestimated.

Quite rightly, sitting is considered to be one of the 'high school' circus tricks and, in performances, a sitting horse often becomes the audience's favourite. There is something special about a horse that is sitting – you can see the pride in his eyes, which may well be due to the fact that he is infected with our enthusiasm.

Sitting can be effectively combined with many other tricks. You could, for example, teach your horse to wave, using the Spanish walk, or fan a cloth between his teeth. Let your imagination run free.

Making an *i*mpression

The Spanish walk comes from a horse's natural inclination to show off, and this exercise and its variations can really make an impression. The Spanish walk has its origins, as the name suggests, in Spain, where it is used in traditional bull fighting to provoke the bull.

The basics and skills required for the Spanish walk.

The Spanish walk is an exercise that draws on a horse's fighting and playing instincts. The horse stretches up each front leg in turn as high as possible, until it almost reaches the horizontal point. Both stallions and mares will strike out with the front legs when playing and fighting, and the further development of this naturally expressive behaviour can be enriching for a horse. It strengthens self-confidence and can be used to release pent-up aggression or cheekiness.

The normal sequence of steps is maintained in the Spanish walk, although sometimes you will see the walk take on a slightly diagonal movement, which is due to the delay in the front leg being set down again. When the Spanish walk is performed correctly, the horse tenses his stomach and pelvic muscles, and collects. The real collection in the perfect Spanish walk is primarily responsible for the suppling effect of this exercise. It is only the weight being

The Spanish walk gives a horse confidence and, when done correctly, encourages freedom through the shoulder.

set back on the hindquarters that allows the horse to lift and stretch his forelegs, so that the Spanish walk can unfold and contribute to greater freedom through the shoulder.

To prepare for the Spanish walk, your horse needs to have a well-established rhythm in the walk and some ability to collect. If this is not the case, he won't be able to string more than one or two steps of Spanish walk together. If he can't transfer his weight back onto his hindquarters he will not have enough freedom through the shoulder and will fall onto his forehand, which will make it virtually impossible for him to lift his forelegs high. Added to this is the inability to work through from behind, which can make the horse appear to be longer in the body than he is and means the exercise can only be performed incorrectly.

The right timing

The Spanish walk is generally considered to be a good introduction to circus work. It very much depends on the individual horse as to whether this reputation is really deserved. Whenever you train your horse to perform a new exercise, you are not just teaching him the movements but also the sentiment behind them. The Spanish walk is a dominant and aggressive movement, which makes it less suitable for young and/or dominant horses, especially stallions. Additionally, it is less suited to inexperienced trainers as an introductory exercise. It is sensible to have learned the other in-hand exercises before beginning to teach the Spanish walk.

'Do something with your legs'

The first step is to start with touching exercises, which will later lead to the shoulder lifting and the forelegs stretching out. Stand slightly to the side of your horse, far enough away that he can't accidently hit you with his front leg, but close enough so that you can easily touch him with your whip. Ensure your horse has no fear of your whip by stroking his leg carefully with it.

Now gently touch the foreleg closest to you with the whip. Begin on the cannon bone. Vary the strength, frequency and where you touch the whip on the leg. Try to find the place where your horse reacts the most – this can vary from horse to horse. There will be at least one spot on your horse's foreleg where he will show some form of reaction, be it the slightest twitch of

*C*hecklist

Skills required for the Spanish walk

- Respect for, but no fear of, the whip
- An established rhythm in the walk
- Ability and readiness to collect
- Only suitable for horses as an introductory exercise if they respect their handler

Touching the legs with the whip should result in them being lifted.

a muscle. Reinforce any reaction: a twitch, stamp of the leg, shifting of weight – it doesn't matter what or in which direction. The horse simply needs to learn that he has to do something with his legs.

At the same time, as you are rewarding the horse with your voice and a treat for his reaction, you also need to take away the whip. Then do the same again, placing your whip where you obtained the reaction last time, and praising the horse if he moves his leg. Your horse will soon learn he is sup-

posed to lift his leg when you touch him with your whip.

Next of all you need to establish the place where you will (in the future) give the aid for the Spanish walk. The outside of the cannon bone isn't suitable if your horse has already learned the one-legged bow, or if you are planning to teach him this in the future. The top of the leg or the shoulder are both well suited, as this will mean you can later give the same aid for the ridden Spanish walk. Over time, move

the aid to the chosen place, bit by bit, gradually edging your way towards it.

At this stage of training you can also, if you wish, introduce a voice command. It isn't absolutely necessary but won't do any harm. The voice command should be actively encouraging and be given just before you give the whip aid. Short, concise words are ideal, such as 'Allez', as these can be used in rhythm with the walk. By keeping to the order of 'voice command – whip aid – correct reaction – praise', your horse will quickly learn that the voice command equals the start of the exercise.

Lifting the shoulder and stretching out the leg at a halt

Once your horse reliably lifts up his leg when you touch it on the right spot, you need to get him to move it in the right direction. He should not just randomly move his leg, but instead clearly move it forwards. You therefore need to sort out

Here you can see a keen pupil expressively lifting his shoulder at a halt. At this stage, the horse doesn't need to raise his leg quite so high.

those movements going in the right direction from those going the wrong way. Praise your horse when he lifts his leg up and forwards, even if it is only slightly. Ignore any movement which goes backwards or to the side. At the start you should be satisfied with even the smallest of steps, and always praise every movement forwards. As soon as your horse has understood what you want of him, because of your much targeted praise and rewards, he will be spurred on to taking bigger steps.

In most cases your horse will stretch his leg more the higher he lifts it. Some horses, however, tend to lift their forelegs with a 90 degree angle at the knee. This might look spectacular but, in terms of its suppling effect, it is not as effective. It is only by lifting and stretching the forelegs that the muscles and ligaments in the shoulder

To give your horse a better idea of lifting and stretching his leg you could, if necessary, use a leg rope.

and upper leg and, in particular, the elbow are stretched optimally.

If, after plenty of practice, your horse still won't stretch out his legs of his own accord (and don't be too impatient!) you can add in an intermediate step. You will need a thick, soft rope or a leg rope, which you tie around the pastern. If you want your horse to lift his left leg, hold the end of the rope in your left hand and the whip in your right.

Touch the horse's leg with your whip as usual, waiting until the horse lifts his leg, and then pull the leg gently forwards with your left hand so that it stays stretched. Praise your horse and then allow the leg back down to the ground. Whatever you do, do not lift the leg so high that you start to feel resistance. Your horse should realise you want him to stretch his leg out and forwards. If you have done this correctly he should soon understand what it is you want of him.

As soon as your horse responds to your touch by moving his leg, start to do this preliminary exercise on the other leg as well. This will help to avoid the muscles developing on one side more than the other. At first, change sides so you are always slightly in front of and at an angle to the leg you are asking the horse to move, but ensuring that you are out of reach of his forelegs. Later, however, you should stay on one side and give the aids for both legs from there. On both sides practice getting each leg to move with the horse standing still. This is important so that when the horse starts to walk forward you won't end up between his front legs.

Many horses try to lift their legs up as high as possible. At this stage of training, this doesn't offer any benefits in terms of their physical development, especially with younger horses. Quite the contrary: due to the amount the forehand has to be lifted without really involving any real collection, the horse will lower his thoracic spine and hollow his back. The horse will quickly get used to assuming this incorrect outline, which later you may have problems cor-

The Polka is ideal for preparing the horse for the demands of the Spanish walk. He learns to step through from behind, whilst distinctly lifting his forelegs. At the start you forget about the amount of stretching and the height to which the legs are lifted.

recting. You should ensure the horse's outline remains correct, with the head just in front of the vertical and the hindlegs standing square and not too far apart. Don't practice this 'lift and stretch' too much in the halt but start on the Polka as soon as possible, even if your horse hasn't yet been able to lift his leg up horizontally. If you need to polish up the way your horse lifts his shoulder and stretches up his leg, or correct poor action, it is better to go back to

the Spanish greeting (refer to page 114) which you can commence, once your horse has learned the Spanish walk.

The Polka

The Polka is often seen as the precursor of an accomplished Spanish walk. In the Polka, the horse maintains the footfall and timing of the walk and clearly lifts one front leg higher in a three-time rhythm. The sequence of steps for the forelegs would therefore be 'right high – left – right – left high – right – left' and so on. What is important is the distinct lifting up of the required foreleg. The horse has to learn to stay slightly collected, while keeping the rhythm and finding his balance. Stand at an angle in front of your horse and touch his right foreleg. Your horse should lift up and stretch his leg, as you have already taught him in the last stage. Praise your horse when he does this correctly. Now ask him to take two steps forward and then ask him to lift and stretch his left foreleg and then walk forward with his right and left forelegs. If your horse still doesn't get the stretching part of this exercise, but rather just puts the leg back down in the same place, it's not a disaster and is quite normal. After doing several repetitions, you will need to take some action to get him to put the leg in front of the other one.

To do this, hold the rein or lead rope with one hand close to the halter so you can better control the forward movement. Ask for the leg to lift and stretch, and then give some form of gently forward impulse through the halter. Also ensure you move your body forwards to make it easier for the horse to follow the movement. Touch the appropriate leg just before the horse lifts his leg, which will help make him lift and stretch it more. Giving the aids at exactly the right time is hugely important here. If your horse reacts as you want him to, give him lots of praise. Ask him to take two steps and then do the same on the other leg. Work as slowly as you can. The slower the horse can carry out these movements,

the better. This will mean that he has plenty of time to consciously co-ordinate his movement.

It is important the horse also learns to come through from behind and maintains a slight collection. If your horse leaves his quarters behind, ask a helper to lightly touch his hindlegs to move through, making sure they keep in the correct rhythm with the forelegs. With time, the movement will become smoother so you will be able to cover longer stretches in the Polka. It isn't important that the horse stretches his forelegs out particularly high, but rather that the steps are emphasised. Height will come with practice and the use of targeted praise. If you force the horse to try and lift his leg up high now you could cause the same sort of damage as we discussed with the lifting of the shoulder.

The first proud steps

Once your horse has mastered the Polka you can then start on the Spanish walk. With appropriate preparation this should not cause you or your horse any great problems. It is too much to expect your horse to go straight into lifting and stretching each alternate leg while walking forward. First of all practice lifting and stretching each alternate foreleg from a standstill. Then begin as with the Polka. Stand at an angle to your horse and ask for the Polka. Go very slowly so that your horse can see what you are doing. After one or two Polka steps,

An exemplary Spanish walk with the hindleg stepping well through.

as soon as he has lifted and stretched up a leg, touch the opposite leg immediately afterwards and ask for this one to be lifted and stretched. In most cases the horse will react instinctively and follow your instruction. Then of course you need to give him lots of praise. Try to repeat this supposed fluke and praise your horse every time he reacts. Here too it really isn't important how high the horse lifts his leg, but rather that the steps are carried out distinctly and with expression.

If your horse doesn't understand that he needs to lift his forelegs up alternately without that in-between step you will need to take things even more slowly. Ask the horse to lift and stretch the right foreleg and ask him forward and then immediately ask the left foreleg to do the same, just as before. Now ask for a couple of normal walk strides and then repeat it all over again until your horse has grasped it.

A further way of encouraging even and rhythmic alternating steps is to develop the

Spanish walk on one side only. This means that you restrict your training of the Spanish walk to one side only. Position your horse on the outside track of your arena; ask the inside leg for Spanish walk and for a normal stride on the outside. Then ask again for one stride of Spanish walk on the inside leg and a normal stride on the outside. Practice this until your horse can do this smoothly. Then change sides and do the exercise on the other rein until he can perform it well on this side too. Now it is time to ask for two connected strides of Spanish walk, one on each side, rewarding any attempt at doing it correctly. At the start do not ask for more than two connected strides and then put in a short phase of walk of six to eight strides, before starting over again. This way you will prevent your horse from falling out through the hindquarters or onto the forehand which would make it impossible for him to perform the Spanish walk correctly. Once you have managed two steps well, try to gradually increase the number. If after much practice your horse can still not do more than four consecutive strides in Spanish walk without losing his balance or impulsion then go back a stage and work on the Polka again.

The Spanish greeting

When riding the Spanish walk it is the reins that will ask for the foreleg to lift and stretch. There is another exercise that will help you to towards this – the Spanish greeting. Here the horse lifts his foreleg in exactly the same way as in the Spanish walk, but holds it there and sets it back

The importance of the hindlegs

The energy with which the hindlegs are lifted off the ground when stepping forward is very important. The height of the forelegs isn't determined by stronger touching nor by your encouragement to stretch, but rather through the horse's balance being shifted back more onto his hindquarters. If your horse steps more through from behind he will be able to stretch his forelegs higher without losing rhythm or hollowing his back. Performing this exercise correctly is vital for maintaining your horse's health. With time, the sequence of steps in the Spanish walk will become almost diagonal in nature: the left foreleg and the right hindleg will start to land on the ground at almost the same time. This is not a mistake but rather the result of the delay of the foreleg coming back down, due to it stretching and taking longer to land.

For the Spanish greeting the horse lifts and holds one foreleg horizontally until the command is given to the exercise.

down only on command. You horse will therefore need to learn the rein aid for the Spanish walk and later the leg and weight aids too.

From now on your horse will need to wear a bridle. Don't use a drop noseband and fasten his noseband loosely, so he can chew his treat rewards and be receptive to your aids. If your horse has a thick mane it is a good idea to plait it, so you can concentrate on what you are doing rather than have to continuously avoid getting tied up in the excess hair!

First of all, your horse has to learn to lift up his leg when you lift each respective rein. Position yourself slightly to the left side of the horse's shoulder and hold the left rein in your left hand, just under the horse's chin. Clearly lift the rein up and touch your horse's leg on the accustomed place. Since your horse already knows what he is supposed to do, he will lift and stretch his foreleg. Praise your horse at the exact moment he shows any sign of responding correctly.

If your horse responds by offering a step of Spanish walk and moves forwards, don't punish him but rather correct him by asking him to step back again. When giving the aid, hold the rein carefully but firmly to prevent him moving forward. If this doesn't work, position yourself next to a fence or on the outside track next to the rails – your position in front of him at an angle should also prevent him from moving forward. Ensure you are out of reach of his fore-legs. This will make you less flexible in the way you give the aids, so do not stay in this position for too long.

Practice getting the foreleg to lift as a reaction to giving the rein aid on the same side, several times in succession. Give the voice command, lift the rein and touch the leg on the same side, and wait for your horse to react. Don't forget to praise him and offer him a treat. Your horse should quickly connect the rein being lifted with him lifting his foreleg.

Up until now you should have been satisfied with the horse lifting the appropriate leg for a moment only. Now you need him to hold his leg up until you finish giving the aid. If your horse wants to put the leg back down, ask again with the rein and touch his leg with the whip while giving the voice command. If your horse hesitates for even a second, praise him. He will probably still put the leg down, but then ask for the same leg to be lifted up again. Shorten the time as much as possible between the application of the aids, until the rein and touching aid become continuous without being reapplied. It will not take long until your horse realises he is not supposed to set the leg back down at all.

At first your horse will not be able to hold his leg still when stretching it horizontally, but is likely to start waving or paddling it about. Don't worry about this, but just sep-

If you intend to ask for a ridden Spanish walk then you can use the Spanish greeting to help establish the correct aids through the reins.

arate out the correct from the incorrect. Praise him when he moves the leg less and ignore it when he waves the leg about too much.

Over time you can reduce the use of the whip to a stage when you only need it to clarify or reinforce your aids when the horse doesn't react to the rein being lifted. In the last stage of training, move from giving the rein aid close to the horse's mouth to above the horse's neck, at the point where you would normally hold your reins when riding.

You could have introduced this step when you were teaching the horse to lift his shoulder and leg. I have intentionally chosen to place it at this stage, because using just the reins without the appropriate aids given from the saddle causes most horses to lose their balance. At best, the horse will lose his rhythm, but more likely still is that he will fall out through the quarters. We will then risk the horse dropping on to his forehand, which we have been trying so hard to avoid. For this reason I have intentionally waited to introduce the use of the reins until this point.

The ridden Spanish Walk.

Often the Spanish walk makes the most impact when performed with a rider. Only then is it possible to give enough attention to every detail. The rider contains the horse with his aids so that the Spanish walk can be performed to perfection. Due to the training already done in-hand, performing the Spanish walk with a rider should not cause you any problems.

Do give your horse time to get used to the new situation and the change of balance needed. It is sensible to get help from a second person. This person should sit passively in the saddle and allow him- or herself to just be carried until the horse has re-established his rhythm and confidence with the additional weight, while you give him the customary aids from the ground.

To teach the horse to perform the Spanish walk with a rider, repeat the same steps from the saddle as you used when training from the ground. Begin by asking the horse to lift his shoulder and leg in the halt, then ask for the Spanish greeting with the already established rein aids. The rider needs to have great co-ordination and sensitivity to be able to give the aids for the Spanish walk correctly. In addition to the rein aids, you also need to give the correct leg aids and aids through the seat. It is tempting to use your leg on the same side as you want the horse to lift his on. This is incorrect. Just as with the walk, you need to use your leg to ask for the appropriate hindleg to move through from behind and underneath the horse's centre of gravity. You need to apply your leg just as the hindleg on the same side swings through from behind. In practice, an example of this would be that you apply your left leg, which causes your horse to step forward with his left hindleg. At virtually the same time, you lift the right rein. You are therefore pushing your horse through from one leg into the opposite hand. By lifting the rein, you are asking your horse to take a stride of Spanish walk, while the other aids help to contain and frame the horse.

Providing the horse is happy to lift his shoulder and leg at the halt, you can ask for single steps in Spanish walk. Keep on the

The ridden Spanish walk: Begin by asking the horse to lift his shoulder when at a halt to help him understand the unaccustomed aids …

… until you can apply them to the work in walk.

outside track and ask your horse to lift his inside foreleg. Praise him and then allow him to walk on again. Repeat this exercise on both reins.

Next, ask your horse to walk markedly slower than usual. Halt, ask for a single step of Spanish walk, and immediately walk on. If your horse manages this without any problems, you can skip the halt and ask for single steps of Spanish walk on the inside leg while walking normally. Go through the same process with the outside leg and then repeat this sequence on both reins. Reduce the number of steps, so you are doing something similar to the Polka,

which you performed before in-hand. If you manage this the next logical step is the full Spanish walk. At the start, do not ask too much of your horse – two steps are quite enough. Give him frequent opportunity to relax and stretch in walk and trot. To improve the engagement of the hindquarters you can use the rein back, immediately followed by several steps of Spanish walk.

Special versions of the Spanish walk

The special versions of the Spanish walk – the Spanish walk backwards and the Spanish trot – place extremely high demands on the co-ordination of both horse and rider. So much so, that they are usually reserved for professionals only. However, I do not want to avoid mentioning them and include them as an added incentive, in case you would like to engage in a greater challenge for both you and your horse.

The Spanish walk backwards
The Spanish walk performed backwards requires an even greater engagement of the hindquarters than the ordinary Spanish walk does. To teach the horse to perform this movement, go back to the exercise when you ask him to lift his shoulder and leg up. Ask him to lift and stretch his leg, but then encourage him to walk back a step after putting the leg down again. Given time your horse will understand that he should step back as he sets the leg down. Then you can give the aid to back up at the

!

Praise from the saddle

Don't forget to offer your horse plenty of praise from the saddle. If you would usually give him treats and don't have a helper on the ground, just offer him the treat and if necessary, turn his head round towards you. Your horse will quickly understand where to get his treat from and soon you won't need to show him.

The ridden Spanish trot – with a little assistance from a helper.

same time as you are asking the foreleg to lift. Praise even the smallest sign of the horse putting that foreleg down further back, at the start asking for only a single step at a time. Over time you can gradually ask for more steps.

The Spanish trot

This movement is similar to Passage, with the forelegs stretched out more and lifted higher. From a highly collected trot, the horse is given the Spanish walk aid and encouraged to lift one leg higher. At the start, as usual, be satisfied with single steps until you are able to perform several steps of Spanish trot in succession. This can also be used to work towards Passage. You can, of course, work in the opposite direction and use the Passage to train the Spanish trot.

A selection from our **b**ox of tricks

As well as the classical circus tricks, there is a wide range of other tricks that you can work on with your horse. Here we are looking at having fun learning together, rather than thinking about improving suppleness. These exercises are a great way of giving your horse a new challenge, as he will need to really use his brain. To train these types of tricks, an important prerequisite is an understanding of the basics of how a horse learns, and in particular operant conditioning (refer to page 22). The use of a clicker is not absolutely necessary but tends to make training considerably easier.

Crossing the legs

Crossing the legs is one of the most loved tricks, as it is fairly easy to learn and looks both charming and showy. The horse crosses one foreleg over in front of the other and moves his weight to the middle, so he is standing on both legs evenly, and then stays in this position.

Some horses will have a particular talent for crossing their legs. Horses that are supple as well as those that have already done some circus trick work will be likely to find this much easier than 'newbies' do, purely because of their greater mobility. Horses with relatively short, thick legs or broad chests will be at a disadvantage, since they will find it more strenuous to fully bring one leg across the other. You should not forget that, as easy as this exercise

There are many ways to teach a horse to cross his legs: by moving him sideways ...

... using contact ...

... or by giving him a little helping hand.

might look, it requires great concentration from the horse and a great deal of co-ordination from horse and trainer.

Before you start with the exercise itself, you should check that the horse is happy to be stroked around his front and on his legs with both the whip and your hand, without becoming unsettled. Since this exercise also requires you to stand close to the forelegs you need an absolutely reliable horse, so you avoid any injuries.

Version 1: stepping sideways

This version assumes your horse has already learned to cross over his legs either through being asked to move across sideways or through knowing how to do a turn on the haunches (demi-pirouette). This makes it relatively easy to then teach him to cross his forelegs over and stand with his legs crossed.

Let's assume you are standing on your horse's near side, either sideways (looking at his neck) or slightly turned towards the horse at an angle to his shoulder. Hold the lead rope close to the head collar with your left hand, and put your right hand on your horse's shoulder. Ask your horse to cross one leg over in front by moving the lead rope across and pushing gently on his shoulder, rewarding him at exactly the moment when he crosses his near foreleg over the off foreleg.

Some horses are quite happy to stand with crossed legs after this first step, which is really hitting the jackpot and deserves lots of praise and treats. Most horses will, however, immediately move back to the starting position before you get a chance to give a reward. That's not bad and the horse should still get his treat. Initially what you are trying to do is teach the horse that he gets a reward for crossing his legs. You need to reinforce this with verbal praise at the right moment too.

After the horse has willingly crossed his legs over a few times, he needs to keep them crossed. This is best achieved by blocking his backwards movement immediately after he has crossed his legs by gently holding onto his headcollar and/or shoulder, the precise timing being essential. When you can see that your horse has remained in position with his legs crossed for even one solitary second, reward him immediately and finish the exercise. You then delay giving him his treat and gradually increase the delay. It is only a matter of time before your horse will be prepared to remain with crossed legs for longer. In the meantime, the reward acts as a signal that the exercise is over. Later, you can (if you wish) replace this with a voice command or different signal to indicate the end of the exercise. It doesn't matter if your horse's legs are crossed closely together or with one leg further forward.

As soon as he has understood what it is that you want of him, you can change the aids. Easiest of all is to start pressing gently on his shoulder with your hand and gradually reduce the aids given through the head collar. If this works, you can change your position so you are looking in the same direction as the horse. Last of all you can, if you wish, cross over your own legs over and use this as the only signal for the exercise. To do this you must cross your own legs and possibly also give a voice command as the first aid, until these are enough to prompt your horse to cross his legs.

Version 2: responding to touching

Another way of getting there is working with touch. For this method, your horse should already have learned to lift his leg after being touched and also, ideally, be happy for his leg to be lifted up.

Stand on the near side at your horse's shoulder, with the whip in your right hand. The left hand, as in the previous version, holds the lead rope close to the head collar. Now touch the outside of the cannon bone until the horse lifts his leg. If he reacts correctly, give him his reward. The next step is to touch him on his cannon bone again and, with your left hand, move his head so he is encouraged to transfer his weight forwards and to the right. The horse should ideally try to put his near foreleg down slightly in front of the off foreleg.

Once the horse has understood and learned to accept the whip as giving him the direction (in other words, when touched on the outside of his cannon bone this means moving the leg away from the whip and putting it down in front of or sideways across the other foreleg), the rest is just a matter of time. As always, at the start you should be happy with a small achievement. If you manage to motivate your horse he will cope with this exercise happily and will quickly make progress. Once your horse is standing with his legs crossed, try to draw out giving him his reward. It can be helpful to silently count the seconds. It is important to give him his reward before he uncrosses his legs of his own accord.

As the last step you can then, as explained in version one, introduce a different command to initiate the exercise.

Version 3: a helping hand

Another common method is using your hand to help the horse cross his legs. The problem with this is that you are doing the exercise for the horse. You are putting the horse in the desired position without making him aware of how he does it himself. This can lead to the horse getting upset and trying to get himself out of an unfamiliar position, and in doing so he could possibly hurt himself or you. However, with a quiet, laid-back horse whose conformation isn't ideal for this exercise, this method is a possible option.

Lifting

Lifting and carrying are much loved tricks, as well as being among the fundamentals of trick training in general. Nearly every horse can learn to do this, but as always

It is quick and easy to make your own pyramid from bits of hose and some rope. You can also find suitable dog toys in your local pet store, even plastic carrots that squeak when an animal bites into them, and your horse will be able to carry these ...

When practicing carrying, choose an object your horse will find easy to grasp between his teeth.

some horses are especially well suited. Usually young horses or stallions feel the urge to nibble or bite into anything their teeth can get hold of. These horses learn to carry objects particularly easily, simply by reinforcing their natural behaviour.

So, what do you do when you have a horse that doesn't have this natural talent? When starting out, use an object that is easy to pick up and lift. I use a home-made pyramid consisting of bits of garden hose, but you should be able to find something in your local pet store that has been designed for dogs, or even a hand towel can serve the purpose well.

First of all, condition your horse to touching the object by praising any contact it makes with it until your horse has understood that he is supposed to touch it. Do this by holding out the object to your horse and once he is used to it, put it down on the ground. Practice him touching the object again. Once the horse is happy to touch the object, we have to shape his behaviour so the horse touches the object with his mouth, and better still with his lips – only then should you praise him. The horse will quickly understand this, as

long as you only reward him when he actually touches the object and not when you think he has touched it.

At some stage it will occur to your horse that he shouldn't just touch the object, but also pick it up. Experiment a little with praise and stretch it out until you give him his reward. Encourage your horse to hold the object in his mouth and don't give the reward immediately. In the expectation of the reward your horse will get impatient and try out what he can do to receive his reward. Normally, most horses quickly start to nibble on the object and play with it with their lips. As soon as this happens, reward the horse.

By praising only when the horse opens his mouth and then later only when he touches the object with his teeth, you can start to mould his behaviour and teach him to bite it. Only praise your horse when he actually bites the object. You can hasten this stage of the process by smearing the object with honey, syrup or something similar.

It can take a while until the horse really bites into the object, depending on how keen he is. If the horse is not particularly enthusiastic, go back to the previous step and start again.

Lifting the object will happen at some stage by itself. Once the horse has understood that he is supposed to hold the object in his mouth, offer him his reward at stomach height. Your horse will quickly understand where to get his treat and finally lift his head with the object still in his mouth.

When the horse is happy to consistently lift up an object, you can then swap the object with other things. This also helps to reinforce his behaviour again.

Carrying

Carrying is no different from advanced lifting and will only work once the horse has lifting off pat. Ask the horse to lift up an object and put it in your hand, by placing your hand at a point just underneath his nose. Praise your horse when the object reaches your hand. If your horse now lets it go, that's fine. When he can do that you could then position yourself so that he has to move his hand in order to give you the object. Tempt your horse towards you. If he lets the object go before it reaches your hand, start over again.

Once this works, you can widen the distance between you and your horse so that he has to take several steps with the object in his mouth. This stage requires good

Carrying is simple to learn with a light, easy to carry object.

timing as well as a period of time. Experience has shown that a horse finds it difficult to walk when carrying an object in his mouth.

When he can do it though, extending the distance is just a question of time and training.

Undressing

I would like to teach you how your horse can learn to take off your jacket, as an example of the funny tricks that can be developed out of lifting and carrying. Your horse is supposed to hold your jacket by the collar and pull it off you, if possible holding onto it and not letting it drop.

For this trick, it is best to use a stout, old jacket or a gilet with a collar, so the horse can hold on to it better. Once again, you need to condition your horse to the jacket and teach him to take it either out of your hand or lift it up from the ground and hold onto it. In the case of more advanced horses that are good at carrying, you could quickly move to getting your horse to give you your jacket to put on. The greater the range of objects your horse has learned to lift up or to carry, the more quickly he will learn this trick.

Once the horse has understood that he has to pick up the jacket and hold on to it, you could place it across your shoulders (but don't put your arms through the sleeves yet), turn your back to your horse, then put your hands behind you and grab

After plenty of practice and with the support of a clicker, taking your gilet off really isn't that hard.

onto the collar to encourage your horse to grab the jacket there. I would recommend you praise the horse when he bites into the jacket collar, so that the horse learns he needs to hold on to the collar and not the back or the arm of the jacket. Most horses will hold on firmly at this stage, until you take the jacket away from them.

Next put one arm through the sleeve, usually the one closest to the horse, since you will then be able to turn towards the horse and use the other hand to assist. Encourage the horse to take hold of the jacket. The horse should grab hold of the jacket as he has already been taught – if not, you will have to repeat the previous steps. If the horse grabs hold of the jacket you will probably have to turn and pull yourself out of the jacket, but soon the horse should be able to tug the jacket off your arm using his own strength. If it works with one arm, you can put on the jacket completely and ask your horse to take it off you again.

The difficulty in this exercise lies not in

Perfect: at the end of the exercise, the gilet is handed back to the trainer.

teaching the horse how to do it, but rather teaching it so that he does it with enjoyment but doesn't then try to do it unasked at every opportunity. It is best, especially in the beginning, to only use one specific jacket for this exercise. If the horse nevertheless starts to tug at any jacket you are wearing, turn away or put yourself out of reach and ignore the behaviour. If that doesn't help then you can clearly say 'no' in a warning tone or give the horse a small tap.

Imaginative variations

Using the same training principles as with lifting, carrying and taking off a jacket, countless other tricks can be invented and developed – for example stealing a hat off your head, carrying a basket or pulling off a rug.

Flehmen, yawning and other behaviours

Teaching horses to perform certain gestures or behaviours on command is really popular. To do this, however, there have to be enough opportunities to positively reinforce any given behaviour. The horse has to show the flehmen reaction or yawn several times, so that we can identify an associated signal with which to control it. You have to carefully observe when he shows specific types of behaviour.

It is usually quite easy to teach stallions and sometimes geldings to show the flehmen response. Stallions often do this when they smell a mare's urine or when they sense unusual, stimulating smells. It is then quite easy to reward the horse as soon as he shows this response, at the same time as giving the chosen voice command.

A clever trick: the Flehmen on command.

If you repeat it often, the behaviour will be quickly established and you will be able to call it up on command.

For horses that don't so readily show the flehmen response it will be more difficult. Tickle your horse on his upper lip with the end of the whip or a feather and reward him immediately if he curls his lip up, even slightly. Build on this, always giving the horse a reward at the right time and give the treat itself from a higher and higher position so that it almost looks like a 'genuine' flehmen response. Another possibility is to position a treat in such a way that the horse has to lift his upper lip to reach it.

With positive reinforcement, almost all gestures may be commanded, including the yawn. Yet more impressive is when a voice command such as 'Are you tired?' is sufficient to trigger yawning.

Saying yes and no

When saying yes, the horse moves his head up and down so that it looks as if he is nodding in the affirmative. Saying no is nothing more than him shaking his head on command. Both exercises are relatively simple to teach and are usually easily and willingly performed by most horses. It is also quite possible your horse will do this exercise without being asked, so you should carefully weigh up whether you can live with this. You should be able to contain the risk by using control signals, but you won't be able to switch it off completely.

Gentle tickling on the breast evokes in most horses a nodding of the head.

Saying yes

Use a toothpick or something similar with which to imitate a fly tickling your horse's chest. Some horses react to this by nodding their heads. If this is the case with your horse, all you have to do is reinforce this reaction and introduce a related command or signal for you to be able to initiate it in the future. You can use a signal such as tapping the horse on the chest or underneath his neck.

If your horse doesn't react to the tickling, you will have to find another way of getting there. Hold a treat in your hand and get your horse to follow it with his mouth. Move your hand upwards and reward the horse if he follows your hand. Move your hand down and again praise your horse when he follows your hand. Then start over again. After several attempts your horse should be so conditioned to your hand that he will follow it without it containing treats. If not, you could add treats in every now or then to give him a bit more enthusiasm for the exercise.

Working this way, you could use a hand movement to ask for the horse to say yes. You could, of course, use a less obvious signal such as tapping his chest or neck as suggested above. Do this before you move your hand up and down in the air so that the horse can connect the two. You can also introduce a voice command. Don't forget to always reward your horse for doing the right thing.

Saying no

Saying 'no' is best taught by tickling the horse on or in his ear with a thin cord tied to the end of whip – sometimes the thong at the end of the whip is suitable for this, especially when is a little frayed. It is surprising how quickly a horse will shake his head when tickled like this – and you should praise and reward this reaction. Before long all you will need to

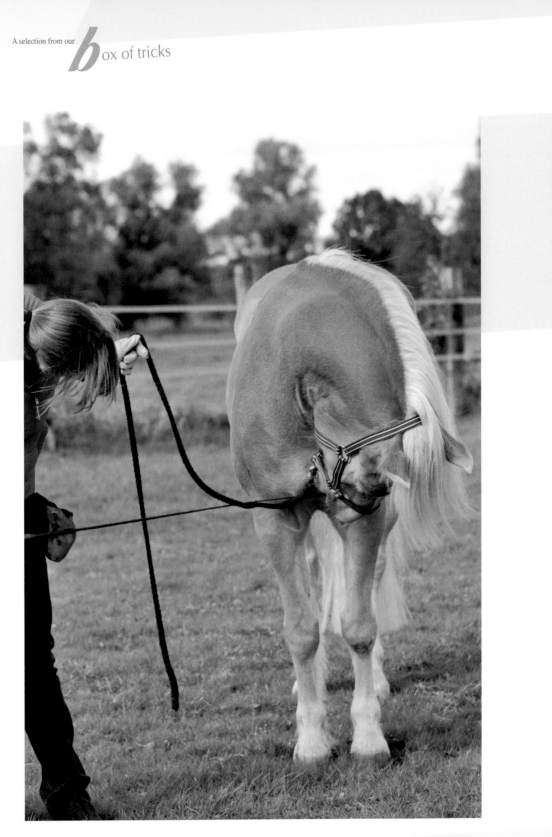

do is give a light tap on the horse's ear for him to shake his head. Then you could and should introduce a voice command and gradually start to extend the distance from which you give the physical aid to the ear, so that in the end all you need to do it point to the ear, rather than having to touch it.

It is important the horse gives up shaking his head every time his ear is touched as soon as possible. You achieve this by every now and then stroking his ears with your

The horse's ear is tickled until he shakes his head.

Soon all you will need to do is point at the horse's ear to get him to shake his head.

hand while asking him to keep still. Alternating this with the command to say 'no' usually works the best, but you should be aware that from now on the horse will associate his ears being touched with shaking his head – so you should seriously consider whether you really want to start with this lesson at all.

A few *final* words

Congratulations! If you and your horse have correctly performed all of the exercises and tricks in this book then you have achieved a lot together. You will now be an experienced partnership and have an impressive repertoire of different exercises.

You will have learned a great deal during your work: about your horse, your shared work, your strengths and weaknesses, and not least about yourself. And you haven't finished yet. Using a bit of creativity and imagination, you should not find it hard to think up your own new tricks and exercises. With trick training in particular, there is an endless number of possibilities for variation. Perhaps you are even attracted by the idea of performing publicly. Believe in yourself and your horse – and use the opportunity to show what you can do.

I have enjoyed being able to accompany you a bit of the way and wish you and your four-legged companion a wonderful time together.

I would like to take this opportunity to thank all those who have accompanied me during this project:

- Cadmos Publishing, who made this book possible;
- Thomas and Sabine Hedtke, as well as the team from the Wüstenkate Stables in Nützen near Hamburg, for allowing us to use their facilities for the photography;
- My photo models Sarah Langmaack with Santano, Kirstin Reese with Sandokan and Mikey, Astrid Witt with Shaman, Fiona Steenbuck with Simba and Welcome, as well as Corinna Scholz with Esperanzador, who all actively supported me during the photography;
- My friends for tirelessly proof-reading my manuscript and their inspiration;
- And naturally my greatest teacher and mentor, my horse Tarek, who carries a large share of the responsibility for this book being written.

Sylvia Czarnecki
February 2011

Appendix

Further reading:

Bea Borelle:
Trick Training for Horses
Vermont: Trafalgar Square Books, 2011

Karen Pryor:
Reaching the Animal Mind: Clicker Training
and What It Teaches Us about All Animals
Scribner Book Company; 2010

Marlitt Wendt:
How Horses Feel and Think: Understanding
Behaviour, Emotions and Intelligence
Schwarzenbek: Cadmos, 2011

Marlitt Wendt:
A Quiet Word with Your Horse: Learning by
Reward – the Key to Motivation and Trust
Schwarzenbek: Cadmos, 2012

Author's contact details:

Sylvia Czarnecki, 42489 Wülfrath
Motionclick.de - Best Behaviour Horse Training,
Circus Training, Natural Horsemanship, Clicker Training
Website: www.motionclick.de
E-mail: info@motionclick.de

Index

CADMOS

HORSE GUIDES

Marlitt Wendt

A Quiet Word with your Horse

It is a magic moment – horse and rider really understand each other for the first time. There is a way to combine communication and effectiveness in one training method with the help of clicker and target. It means the horse-appropriate alternative to common methods based on pressure and dominance. Biologist Marlitt Wendt teaches the mechanism of learning by reward based on the latest perception of the horse´s psyche.

128 pages · Paperback
ISBN 978-0-85788-007-9

Thies Böttcher

Gentle Horse Training

"The rider is the horse's trainer." Adopting this underlying principle to his training, Thies Böttcher shows how to develop your horse's abilities and advance his training. The training approach that is presented in this book can be easily integrated into your training programme, whatever your style of riding is. This book is an inspiring training guide for all those who wish to develop a strong and successful relationship with their horse, without the use of force.

144 pages · Paperback
ISBN 978-3-86127-977-8

Daniela Bolze/Christiane Slawik

My Horse Told Me

With their wide range of expressive behaviours, horses are always full of surprises. These behaviours can range from curious, friendly and insecure to threatening, as a warning of attack. First and foremost, this book trains the horse lover's eye to the communication that constantly takes place between horses, but more importantly between people and horses in their day-to-day dealings with one another.

128 pages · Paperback
ISBN 978-0-85788-013-0

Marlitt Wendt

How Horses Feel and Think

This is a fascinating journey into the emotional world seen from a horse's point of view. The information provided offers a good basis for horse owners to learn how to relate better to their horses, to develop a more harmonious relationship to their horses and to school their horses without using force but in a positive, pro-active way.

128 pages · Paperback
ISBN 978-0-85788-000-0

Renate Ettl

How to Keep Your Horse Calm and Relaxed

For riders who want to handle horses safely and to avoid accidents, a horse must be obedient and respect discipline. This book is not only a guide for safety-conscious riders who want an obedient horse, but also offers advice, plenty of exercises and a profound knowledge of a horse's natural behaviour. Step-by-step, it explains how to train a horse to be a pleasure to own.

80 pages · Paperback
ISBN 978-3-86127-920-4

For more information, please visit:
www.cadmos.co.uk

CADMOS